Yo, Blair!

Yo, Blair!

Geoffrey Wheatcroft

POLITICO'S

First published in Great Britain 2007 by
Politico's Publishing, an imprint of
Methuen Publishing Ltd
11–12 Buckingham Gate
London
SW1E 6LB

1

A CIP catalogue record for this book is available from the British
Library.

ISBN 978-1-84275-206-7

Set in Baskerville by SX Composing DTP, Rayleigh, Essex
Printed and bound in Great Britain by MPG Books Ltd, Bodmin,
Cornwall

Part One:

Leader of the Free World

Prologue: A strong ally

I can go out and just talk

In July 2006, two Prime Ministers came to Washington, one a novice, the other a very familiar visitor. Following the elections only months earlier, Nouri al-Maliki had been appointed Prime Minister of Iraq, personifying that very democratisation of the country which President George W. Bush had proclaimed as a final reason for the invasion in March 2003, after all other ostensible justifications had collapsed. Maliki's visit proved wonderfully embarrassing.

By way of response to Hezbollah rockets – and acting on the Biblical principle 'Saul has slain his thousands, and David his ten thousands' – Israel had launched a devastating attack on Lebanon which laid waste much of the country, provoking angry criticism throughout most of the world and a fresh wave of hatred in all Arab and Muslim countries. While this was happening, Maliki met various politicians in Washington, who told him that he must condemn Hezbollah and express his sympathy for Israel. He declined to do so, and was in turn angrily upbraided, notably by Congressional Democrats who were vying as ever to outdo the Republicans in unconditional support for Israel.

'Unless Mr Maliki disavows his critical comments of

Israel and condemns terrorism,' said Nancy Pelosi, the Democratic leader in the House of Representatives who became Speaker after the midterm elections months later, 'it would be inappropriate to honour him with a joint meeting of Congress.' The Democratic Party chairman, Howard Dean (of all people, not long before a supposedly radical candidate for the presidential nomination), went further, calling Maliki an 'anti-Semite' for his failure to denounce Hezbollah. With a comical candour verging on unconsciousness, Dean said, 'We don't need to spend $200 and $300 and $500 billion bringing democracy to Iraq to turn it over to people who believe that Israel doesn't have a right to defend itself.' Quite so: as Dean was making more clear than he may have realised the invasion had been an exercise in what was once called 'native politics', whose great object was to install a pliable local regime, well disposed toward the United States and Israel.

It had apparently never even occurred to those who proposed the democratisation of Maliki's country, and then of the larger Middle East, that the more democratic most Arab countries were to become, the more Islamist or nationalist they were likely to be (or both), and the more bitterly hostile to Israel and the West; it hadn't struck them even as a possibility that free elections, in Iran or Palestine, were likely to have outcomes highly unpalatable to Washington. Nor had it crossed Dean's mind that 'bringing democracy to Iraq' would indeed turn it over to rulers who admired Hezbollah more than Israel, since that was the sentiment of the *demos* or people. This Maliki seemed to the Americans altogether a very uppity fellow,

4

who was saying not at all the kind of thing they wanted to hear, even if, by criticising Israel, he was merely expressing the views of those who had elected him. That's what democracy is usually supposed to mean.

But help was at hand for America. The next visitor to Washington wasn't uppity at all nor in any way disobedient, and he certainly evinced no similar need to express the views of his electorate: here was a good native politician. In his tenth year as British Prime Minister, Anthony Blair was all that the Bush administration, and those Democrats, could have wished for. From the beginning of his time in office he had worked in close alliance with Washington, even when that contradicted his supposed desire to work more closely with Europe, or when it repudiated existing British policies, not to mention when it ran against obvious British interests or ignored the views of the British people.

He had formed a close political friendship with Bill Clinton before nimbly transferring his allegiance to George W. Bush and, after he had wholeheartedly supported Bush's invasion of Iraq and more generally his policies in the Middle East, it had become almost a platitude to say that Blair was the President's poodle. During an earlier visit to Washington, Bush had been asked at a joint press conference if he thought that word fitted, and Blair interjected, grinning with what's meant to be his boyish charm, 'Don't answer that question!' But now in the summer of 2006, caught off the record and off guard, he had answered it himself.

Shortly before this visit to Washington, President and Prime Minister had gone to St Petersburg when the leaders of the G8 powers met there. They were talking together at the conference table where a microphone had been inadvertently left open (until Blair noticed it with alarm and hurriedly switched it off). It gave a squint into their relationship at once hilarious and excruciating.

A bored and resentful Bush greeted the prime minister with good-natured disdain – 'Yo, Blair!' – and treated him like a put-upon valet, a part Blair played very convincingly, bowing and scraping as he obsequiously offered to help the Americans in the Middle East, in any way they might want: 'I don't know what you guys have talked about, but, as I say, I am perfectly happy to try and see what the lie of the land is . . .' When Bush reminded him that Condoleezza Rice, the Secretary of State, was going there, Blair added in still more revealing words, 'Well . . . it's only if, I mean . . . you know. If she's got a . . . or if she needs the ground prepared, as it were . . . Because obviously if she goes out, she's got to succeed, as it were, whereas I can go out and just talk.'

The Americans did things, Blair just talked, as it were. Maybe manservant wasn't quite the comparison: as Maureen Dowd of the *New York Times* put it with painfully accurate wit, the Prime Minister 'was hovering and wheedling like an abused wife'. Or if Blair truly were Bush's poodle, it would have been a case for the RSPCA.

That grotesque moment in Russia had been a fitting prelude to Blair's American visit. With the violence in Lebanon escalating, Labour MPs were enraged, members of his own Cabinet publicly criticised the excessive use of force by Israel and called for an immediate ceasefire, and – much more to the point – the Israeli action was disapproved by most British people: in one poll, only 22 per cent thought the retaliation in Lebanon was justified. But Blair, all unlike Maliki, refused to join in these criticisms, to voice the feelings of his country, to propose a ceasefire or to diverge in any way at all from the American line that Israel had an unqualified right to defend herself in whatever way she thought best.

Look here, upon this picture, and on this. On the one hand was the Prime Minister of a state which was barely a state and a country which was barely a country, which was a recent invention and an artificial construct in the first place, which had been savaged by years under a brutal dictator and then ravaged by an invasion, which was paralysed by sectarian violence and which stood on the brink of civil war and complete disintegration. But he was still prepared to make some show of national independence as well as personal pride and self-respect. On the other was the Prime Minister of England (as Disraeli among others would have called himself): the leader of a country with a longer continuous existence and national consciousness than almost any on earth, a state which a hundred years before had been something like the global hyperpower, which had uniquely, gallantly and self-sacrificially fought in the two great wars of the twentieth century from very beginning to very end. And he was behaving as if he represented a puppet or satellite, and as if, what's more, he knew it.

'I will never apologise for Britain being a strong ally of the US,' Blair ingratiatingly told a television interviewer on that American visit, quite missing the point as usual. He said that at a time when less than a third of the British people thought that the Iraq invasion had been justified, and nearly two-thirds thought that the Prime Minister was too close to Bush: public opinion which Blair, in contrast to Maliki, was happy to ignore. Most British people had long been well disposed towards the United States and ready to be 'a strong ally' when the White House acted wisely and honestly, though not under any circumstances. Few of the people Blair represented believed in 'my country right or wrong', and they certainly didn't follow his implicit principle when dealing with the Americans, 'your country right or wrong'. The British people thought that Great Britain was on friendly terms with America; until Blair, they didn't realise that it was a client state of Washington.

As Blair's American visit continued, he compounded that impression. Given the grave crisis of the moment there was a case for recalling Parliament and for the Prime Minister to explain himself there, and to his Cabinet, and to his own people in his own country. Instead, he devoted himself to American audiences, before he went off on holiday in the West Indies. After leaving Washington for California he addressed a gathering of Rupert Murdoch's News Corporation at Pebble Beach, giving what Murdoch's *Times* called a 'master-class in leadership'.

This was a reprise. Shortly after he had became leader of the Labour Party in 1994, Blair travelled to Australia to address a News Corp convention, as a guest of Murdoch, the man more hated than any other by the Labour Party. His best-selling tabloid had brutally insulted the Labour leader – 'If Kinnock wins today will the last person to leave Britain please turn out the lights?'

– at the 1992 general election, and had subsequently boasted of the Tory victory in that election that 'it was the *Sun* wot won it'. Speaking in Australia had been one of Blair's first and most eloquent intimations that he was not merely going to turn his back on the party he led, but trample and spit on it.

Twelve years on he told Murdoch's audience in Pebble Beach, who included Clinton and Shimon Peres, the Israeli deputy Prime Minister, that the era of tribal politics was coming to an end, a tired and unoriginal observation though an unhappy turn of phrase in view of events in Iraq, Sudan or even Ulster, where there is still all too much tribalism. In his next speech, in Los Angeles, he said that 'there is an arc of extremism now stretching across the Middle East and touching, with increasing definition, countries far outside that region', not stopping to ask if his own actions might have encouraged that extremism, and added, with an optimism few in his own country shared, that 'it is still possible even now to come out of this crisis with a better long-term prospect for the cause of moderation in the Middle East succeeding'.

Both speeches were not merely given in America, but specifically tailored for American taste. Blair was indeed having a practice run: he has without doubt long been thinking about his future on the lucrative American lecture circuit when he leaves office, as well as the price his memoirs will command with New York publishers, and it is more than possible that this has consciously or unconsciously conditioned his attitude towards the United States.

Then at one more meeting at a college in California he

spoke about global warming, the subject he likes to flourish as a fig leaf whenever accused of mimicking Bush in every field. But even then he couldn't keep off the joshingly sycophantic tone he adopts in America. By way of mentioning another speaker, Blair said with his usual ghastly humour, 'I think, as I was saying yesterday with Governor Schwarzenegger – it is great to be with him. I phoned my wife up and she said to me, "How do you feel being with Arnie Schwarzenegger?" I said, "Actually, I felt acute body envy really." But anyway, we were discussing climate change.'

In another uneasily ingratiating phrase he also told that enthusiastic audience that their warm response was 'quite a difference to the receptions on university campuses I get back home'. It was certainly true that the transatlantic esteem he enjoyed was a contrast with his eclipse at home. His American tours were almost reminiscent of the visit of George IV to Dublin in 1821, where, as the Victorian historian S. R. Gardiner dryly observed, his effusive protestations of affection 'gained him a momentary popularity which was beyond his attainment in a country where he was better known'.

I really believe in it

When Blair had gone to Australia at Murdoch's behest so many years before, his star was still bright in his own country, and remained so well after he won his first election. Nine years later that optimism had been replaced by bitter disappointment and profound disillusionment.

By last autumn not only had the lustre faded, Blair's authority was collapsing under him. Before he won the party leadership he had made one of his many grave tactical mistakes in persuading Gordon Brown to stand aside in the election, instead of challenging him to a clean fight, which Brown could not possibly have won. This supposed agreement poisoned relations between the two men ever after. Then before the 2005 election he made another, when he said he would not serve as Prime Minister for a full term, an adopted Americanism which doesn't belong to British politics, but by which he meant he would be gone before the subsequent election. He thereby inflamed Brown's ambition further and diminished his own position.

That was a bad start, but in some ways Blair's relations with his colleagues, and Labour as a whole, were always destined to be awkward. From when he won his first election onwards, he was what Beaverbrook called Lloyd George, a Prime Minister without a party. Now in the autumn of 2006 his relationship with Brown disintegrated. In the first week of September Brown attempted a coup against the Prime Minister, in blatant fashion, though with characteristic clumsiness, encouraging a rebellion by resignation of junior ministers which went off half-cock, and screaming at Blair during a violent confrontation in Downing Street.

The only result was headlines reading 'Labour paralysed as the poison spreads' and 'Blair clings to the wreckage', but by the end of that bizarre week Brown was clinging to the wreckage as well. At the party conference in Manchester at the end of the month they went out of

11

their way to pay lavish tributes to one another, although while Brown said from the podium what a privilege it had been to work with Blair, the mood was somewhat spoiled when a journalist overheard Cherie Blair spluttering, 'That's a lie.'

A day later Blair's own speech was loudly cheered, but the effect was eerie: not just a Prime Minister without a party, he was now, in another hallowed phrase, in office but not in power – and only in office by the skin of his teeth, beleaguered and unpopular.

All this happened to the only man who had led the Labour Party to three successive election victories, two with huge parliamentary majorities, and whose nearly ten years in office had seen an unprecedented combination of sustained growth and low inflation, unemployment and interest rates. One more well-worn saying holds that all political careers end in failure, but the nature and extent of Blair's personal failure, given how much he had once had going for him, was well-nigh unique.

So was the derision and contempt he now inspired across the country, transcending every division, among young and old, rich and poor, left and right. Once it had been the hard left who loathed Blair, while the middle classes of Middle England had rallied to him. Now a distinguished octogenarian, the emeritus mathematics professor Sir Bryan Thwaites, spoke for very many ordinary people in his unfeigned disgust. Blair's fate should lie not merely with Cabinet and Parliament, he said, but with 'the people of the nation who have been insulted by his behaviour, notably by his recorded conversation with President Bush at the G8 summit. He has so demeaned the great office of Prime Minister that he should go forthwith.'

That bitter resentment among the 'best and brightest' had been simmering well before then, and it is Blair's disastrous foreign policy – or abdication from one – which more than anything explains why he leaves office contemned by so many, and not least by those who had most experience of the conduct of international relations. In the spring of 2004, Blair's servility toward Washington and his unswerving support for the Bush administration in the Middle East had provoked something never seen before, a public protest from dozens of retired ambassadors.

The occasion for the protest was not so much the Iraq war – although that had already proved a predictable calamity, and the supposed reasons for waging it had already been falsified – as one other visit to Washington by Blair, where he was openly humiliated. Bush and Ariel Sharon, the Israeli Prime Minister, cut a deal quite at odds with British policy and presented it to Blair as a *fait accompli*, whereupon he could only whimper that it offered hope for progress. As those veteran diplomatists presciently wrote, 'worse was to come. After all those wasted months, the international community has now been confronted with the announcement by Ariel Sharon and President Bush of new policies which are one-sided and illegal and which will cost yet more Israeli and Palestinian blood.'

But Iraq appalled the Foreign Office also. Although Blair is in no way a radical, he may be thought an outsider or even an anti-establishmentarian in this sense. It has been said, unprovably but very plausibly, that the Iraq war was unwanted by every ambassador in the Foreign Service and every general in the British Army. They bided their time, and then got their own back. In America there has been a 'revolt of the generals', one retired senior officer of the United States Army after another emerging to denounce Donald Rumsfeld for his recklessness and incompetence (not to mention his insulting treatment of the military) and to say things about the debacle in Iraq with a soldierly bluntness heard from almost no American politician. Bluntest was Lieutenant-General William Odom, who earlier last year published an essay in the authoritative journal *Foreign Policy* unambiguously entitled 'Cut and Run? You Bet'.

Although the British generals' memoirs are yet to come they will likely be devastating, but the 'ambos' have already struck, beginning with that letter. Having told us that Bush and Blair were discussing operations against Iraq in September 2001, Sir Christopher Meyer published gossipy but revealing memoirs about his time as ambassador in Washington which made painfully clear the degree of Blair's subservience to Bush. As Jonathan Powell, one of Blair's inner circle of courtiers, had instructed Meyer in New Labour language, 'We want you to get up the arse of the White House and stay there.'

Then in the summer of 2006, a helpfully leaked report to London from William Patey, the departing British ambassador in Baghdad, said, 'The prospect of a low intensity civil war and a de facto division of Iraq is probably more likely at this stage than a successful and substantial transition to a stable democracy.' But most remarkable of all was Sir Rodric Braithwaite, a former

14

ambassador to Moscow and chairman of the Joint Intelligence Committee, as well as author of an admirable history book, *Moscow 1941*, who fired a broadside unparalleled in diplomatic history. 'The Office' has a tradition, if not of absolute loyalty, then of reserve; no more, it seems. It was not merely that the Iraq war had been misbegotten and had turned out disastrously, Braithwaite wrote:

> Mr Blair's prime responsibility is to defend the interests of his own country. This he has signally failed to do. Stiff in opinions, but often in the wrong, he has manipulated public opinion, sent our soldiers into distant lands for ill-conceived purposes, misused the intelligence agencies to serve his ends and reduced the Foreign Office to a demoralised cipher because it keeps reminding him of inconvenient facts. He keeps the dog, but he barely notices if it barks or not. He prefers to construct his 'foreign policy' out of self-righteous soundbites and expensive foreign travel.
>
> Mr Blair has done more damage to British interests in the Middle East than Anthony Eden, who led the UK to disaster in Suez 50 years ago.

That is the nub of it. Blair approaches his tenth anniversary in office, at the end of what looks more and more the most dishonest and disastrous prime minister-ship of modern times. There is a distinction between premiership and government, although Blair has done everything he can to erode it, just as he has relentlessly eroded the traditional boundaries between government, state and party. As a government, the ministry of 1997–2007, quite apart from the state of the economy, may have real achievements to its credit in domestic politics. What so many loathe is the manner of Blair's regime, as so many did of Lloyd George's. He was a politician of greater genius than Blair (and unlike him, a man who led the country successfully in a great war), whose government also had achievements to its credit. And yet, as the historian Kenneth Morgan has written, the Lloyd George government came to be disliked and despised for 'its tone as much as its policies, its atmosphere of intrigue and corruption'.

Those words are horribly apt for a Blair regime which has likewise been poisoned by intrigue and stained by corruption. Lloyd George also was brought down in the end by foreign adventures, as was Eden. Blair has long liked to use a cute turn of phrase when explaining some repressive new measure. He's not just doing it to please the *Sun* or *Daily Mail*, he will say: it's worse than you think, he wants to do it anyway. So it was that he told an interviewer that he would support the Iraq war even if the Americans were opposed (a ludicrous claim, as I shall show): 'It's worse than you think – I really believe in it.'

Those words might stand as an epigraph – or an epitaph – for his career. Lloyd George and Eden were at least undone by pursuing what they, however mis-guidedly, thought the British national interest, but Blair was ruined by pursuing the national interest of another country. His speech to the Murdoch gathering in California ended with a stirring peroration: 'For a leader, don't let your ego be carried away by the praise or your spirit diminished by the criticism and look on each with a very searching eye. But for heaven's sake, above all else, lead.' Never mind the vanity and the slightly deranged language. He hadn't led but been led, and the great, terrible consequence of his years in office is worse than you think: we have ceased to be an independent country.

Straight kind of guy

A thousand days

As Blair approaches the tenth anniversary of his prime ministership and his final departure, his career is in disarray or even in ruins. He will leave shortly, dishonoured and perhaps disgraced. Most of the high hopes held for him ten years ago have been dashed. The achievements of his government at the margins are outweighed by its failures, in its own terms.

Most of the government's record on education, health and crime has been equivocal at best, by its own account: the very fact that Blair never ceases to complain about the state of schools, hospitals and policing, and is still proposing grandiose plans for them, speaks for itself. If the economy has largely prospered, that has only so much to do with the government, and almost nothing to do with Blair himself, who has surrendered economic management – and thus ultimate control of all domestic policy – to Gordon Brown. But even if the most generous possible view is taken of that record, there is a terrible burden of failure and folly on the other side, above all for Blair's most personal contribution: a wrong-headed foreign policy and a disastrous war.

Quite apart from the catastrophe in Iraq, from the very beginning there was a whiff of corruption hanging round the Blair regime, which has since become a stench. The sale of peerages may be the greatest scandal this country has seen for generations, and the investigation moved ever closer to Downing Street until, just before Christmas 2006, the Prime Minister himself was questioned by the police.

And yet with all this, Blair still struts and preens from Washington to Mesopotamia, living in a world of his own, quite unaware of how discredited he is. The word 'denial' is inadequate to describe his condition. He addresses British troops in Iraq and still speaks of a democracy there as the country implodes and his colleagues openly plan withdrawal; he vaingloriously addresses more troops in Afghanistan, while the situation there also deteriorates and a platoon of British soldiers refuses to go on patrol because the ammunition supplied to them by Blair's government is deficient.

At the Labour conference in September 2006 Blair said that during his last months in office he would 'dedicate myself, with the same commitment I have given to Northern Ireland, to advancing peace between Israel and Palestine'. No one has told him that no peace between Israel and Palestine is on offer in any foreseeable future, that the prospects for such a settlement haven't been less propitious for many years, and that there is no person on earth less likely to secure it than the British Prime Minister. This is a man who has lost all contact with reality.

How did this happen? Where, in the phrase, did it all go wrong? How has this come about within ten years of the morning Blair strode into Downing Street on 2 May 1997 amid a mood of exhilaration you could sense in the air? Hindsight is a wonderful thing, but it may be that most of what depresses and even disgusts people about the Blair regime was visible from the start, always adumbrated in his salient characteristics, the trickery and demagoguery, the rhetoric which promised more than it could deliver, the chameleon appeal to all sides at once, the implicit deception.

In one respect the enthusiasts who once rallied to Blair, and the 13.5 million British citizens who originally voted for him, are entitled to speak of disenchantment: no one who voted for Blair's party in 1997, or for that matter in 2001, was voting for war, let alone for a needless and catastrophic invasion of Iraq. His warmongering is the defining quality of his premiership, and the ultimate crime; it was on the battlefield above all that Blair's hubris was followed by nemesis.

And yet in other ways Blair is reminiscent of Carwyn James, the British Lions coach during the 1971 tour of New Zealand, who gave a phrase to sport when he told his team to 'get your retaliation in first'. Many Prime Ministers, especially Labour Prime Ministers, have disappointed and disillusioned their more ardent followers when they took office, with its challenges and necessary compromises. Blair was unique: he got his disillusionment in first. No one who had watched him closely in the period from July 1994, when he became Labour leader, to May 1997, when he became Prime Minister, should have failed to see what he was up to. He began by striking a fundamentally corrupt bargain with the Labour Party, a bargain sealed that first May when 419 MPs were elected and began right away, in their gratitude for salaries and expenses and pensions, to vote for measures they disliked and support ministers they despised.

Many Labour MPs and voters now imply that they were hoodwinked into supporting a man who has been described as standing to the right of every Prime Minister in sixty years apart from Margaret Thatcher, his model and beacon. But they cannot have noticed what he said and did when he became party leader and before he won his first election. The link between him and Thatcher is crucial. Every Conservative leader from Sir Robert Peel onwards agreed in his heart with his opponents that the future belonged with their side; that at best a rearguard action could be fought; that Conservatism's role was to make concessions as slowly, and with as good grace, as possible. That is, until Margaret Thatcher. She was the first Tory leader who did not share this belief.

And Blair agreed with her. He was the first leader of what was ostensibly a party of the left to concede that the right had largely won the argument. As he said, 'I believe Margaret Thatcher's emphasis on enterprise was right.' 'A strong society should not be confused with a strong state.' 'Duty is the cornerstone of a decent society.' 'People don't want an overbearing state.' 'Britain needs more successful people who can become rich by success through the money they earn.' What Tory could have disagreed with any of those sentiments which Blair expressed before 1997? And why would any moderately conservative citizen not have voted for him, at least the once?

But this meant that his party leadership was an exercise in bad faith from the beginning. Here the fascinating comparison is with Disraeli. In her great life of her father, the Prime Minister Lord Salisbury, Lady Gwendolen Cecil writes a devastating passage which applies with remarkable exactness if one only changes the name.

> And in all that is disreputable in Mr Disraeli's [or Blair's] character . . . his lack of scruple as to the methods which he thought permissible is beyond question. He was always making use of convictions that he did not share, pursuing objects which he could not avow, manoeuvring his party into alliances which, though unobjectionable from his own standpoint, were discreditable and indefensible from theirs. It was an atmosphere of pervading falseness, which involved his party as well as himself.

Nothing could improve on that as an account of the way Blair led his MPs, all the way to a war which, though unobjectionable from his own standpoint, was discreditable and indefensible from theirs.

This bad faith applied to Blair's career as Prime Minister as well as party leader: his capacity for deception – beginning with self-deception – was already on display from the start, and helped him once seduce the British people who later came to regard him with such distrust.

Maybe some were impressed when he said, in a BBC television programme interview at the start of his prime ministership: 'I hope the people know me well enough and realise the type of person I am . . . I would never do anything to harm the country or anything improper. I never have. I think people who have dealt with me think I'm a pretty straight sort of guy.' Actually, people who have dealt with Blair, even those who admired him, would more likely admit that, of many terms could be used to describe Blair, 'straight' is the very last word anyone would choose. 'Dicky,' Field Marshal Templer said to Lord Mountbatten, 'you're so crooked that if you swallowed a nail you'd shit a corkscrew.' If that might be going too far with Blair – maybe the nail would only be severely bent – 'straight' is wholly absurd, and would have been at any time of his life, let alone on the occasion which prompted those words.

Just what sort of a guy Blair was had been shown by one episode while he was still opposition leader. In the spring of 1996 a madman called Thomas Hamilton shot dead sixteen children and a teacher in a classroom in Dunblane before killing himself. It was one of those events so horrible and meaningless that no one wise tried to make sense of it. Journalists are inured from what they have to witness by black humour, but there were no jokes among the reporters that day. In a much-relished passage from Evelyn Waugh's *Scoop*, the fraudulent foreign correspondent describes 'a dead child, like a broken doll, spreadeagled in the deserted roadway'; in Dunblane there really were dead children like broken dolls.

When John Major went to visit the grief-stricken town

he displayed the decency of which he was capable by asking Blair as well as Paddy Ashdown to accompany him to Scotland, to show that on occasion they must represent the nation and rise above party. Blair in turn said that it would be quite wrong to make any partisan advantage out of the tragedy, and then proceeded to do exactly that. At the following autumn's Labour conference he made a cheap rabble-rousing speech – including the horrific phrase 'a thousand days to prepare for a thousand years' – in which he effectively blamed the Tories for the massacre of the innocents, and promised a 'total ban on handguns' when Labour came to power.

A law was duly enacted, with entirely predictable consequences: law-abiding citizens were deprived of the right to own small arms for any purpose; British exponents of the Olympic sport of pistol-shooting are obliged to travel abroad to practice their harmless pastime; the ownership of handguns has been confined to two classes: employees of the state and professional criminals; and gun crime has increased throughout Great Britain with every year since the law was passed. All politicians believe instinctively in their omnipotence as well as their omniscience. They can wave a legislative wand and human nature will change: a Labouchere Amendment will mean a 'total ban' on active homosexuality, a Volstead Act will mean a total ban on the consumption of alcohol. The banning of handguns adumbrated the Blair government's addiction to gesture politics, its compulsion for passing laws and creating crimes, and its sheer ineffectuality.

Show us you care

But Dunblane was nothing as compared with 'Diana Week', four months after Blair reached Downing Street. Those bizarre events seem almost dreamlike now, so that the movie *The Queen* takes on as remote and fanciful an historical flavour as *Marie Antoinette*; for that matter, they seemed hallucinatory to some of us at the time. After the death of Princess Diana, ever vaster numbers thronged the Mall day by day, immense quantities of flowers piled up, the mood of the crowd turned unmistakably ugly, egged on by the tabloids. 'Show us you care,' the *Sun* shrieked at the Queen.

A great deal of what already seems breathtaking nonsense was written, now of interest only in what it said about the mood of a nation which could be lulled by Blair's empty rhetoric. For the left-wing playwright David Edgar, Diana Week was 'open, soft, organic and – as the candles lit up London in the small hours of Saturday – turned night into day. It was also, essentially, collective . . . The people who made what Martin Jacques has dubbed the "floral revolution" were engaged in a political act.'

Unlike those supposed men of the left, Edgar and Jacques, some of us felt that we were living in a foreign country or on an alien planet during that week, with its mass hysteria, its Latin-American peasant hagiology, its emotional incontinence. How could anyone feel grief, in the sense felt when a mother dies or a close friend, at the death of a stranger? And yet one man from Leeds said on a radio phone-in, 'My wife died in April . . . and I've shed more tears for Diana than I did for my wife.'

Absurd and embarrassing as this was, Blair was the man to exploit Diana Week, first with his fatuously oxymoronic phrase 'she was the people's princess', then with his harrying of the Queen, insisting that she should return to London to join in the primitive rituals, then when he insisted against all precedent that he should read the lesson at her funeral. *The Queen* gets this wrong, with Blair being asked to read rather than asking: the old courtiers rightly thought that the ceremony should be above politics and that if any parliamentarian read the lesson it should be the Speaker.

But Blair by now would miss no opportunity to manipulate any situation to his advantage, and he duly read the hallowed passage from St Paul's First Epistle to the Corinthians (though in the schmalzy version he inevitably prefers, 'faith, hope and love') in a performance so histrionically hammy that it would have made Sir Henry Irving blush. Tony Blair could always show that he cared.

But there was more to it. That ludicrous phrase 'pretty straight sort of guy' had been prompted by one of the first of the squalid financial scandals which have disfigured the Blair years, scandals which are not some unhappy accident but go the heart of the matter, and the problem with the man himself, beyond any demagoguery and mendacity. Bernie Ecclestone, the maestro of Formula One motor racing, had made a huge donation to Labour, and the new government had then exempted Formula One from an intended ban on cigarette sponsorship. Even an electorate which had recently voted for Blair didn't think that 'straight' was quite the word for that sequence of events.

And it was only the beginning. The past ten years have been punctuated by episodes – Ecclestone, Mittal, Hinduja and finally cash for peerages – for which Blair will be remembered, along with his terrible war. All along he tried, with decreasing plausibility, to explain away this public corruption, with its private roots.

To this day the left have failed to understand or grasp the phenomenon of Blair, but then that's because even now they think instinctively and incorrigibly in ideological terms: they see Blair as having taken over the Labour Party from inside and moved it to the right, which is of course true but misses the deeper truth. The point about 'Blairism' is not that it is ideologically left-wing or ideologically right-wing but that it has no ideological content at all.

Nor would Blair deny that. 'What works' is part of the fatuous New Labour rhetoric, along with 'joined-up government', and he speaks about the redundancy of ideological language and of the concept of left and right, as though these were new insights. In fact it is more than fifty years since the great French political writer Raymond Aron said that 'in most Western societies, the ideological controversy is dying down,' and nearly seventy since Evelyn Waugh, more elegantly than any Blairite, dismissed 'the distinctions of left and right which are now becoming as meaningless and mischievous as the circus colours of the Byzantine Empire'.

It's true that Blair is beyond left and right in the sense of Nietzsche's 'beyond good and evil' (he may be that as well), but his antipathy to any kind of general ideas is not a virtue. Blair has never really understood the failure of state socialism, he just hates the Labour Party. He has never intellectually grasped the case for the competitive market economy, he just loves the rich.

This is one of his most deeply engrained traits. Our pious churchgoing Prime Minister is surely familiar with the liturgy for evensong in the Book of Common Prayer, but by some trick of memory he seems to have inverted the words of the Magnificat. In the Blairite version it goes, 'He hath exalted the mighty in their seats; and put down the humble and meek. He hath filled the rich with good things; and the poor he hath sent empty away.'

It has been said by faltering liberal admirers that Blair may not be a socialist or a radical or a man of the left, but he is not a conservative. That is debatable, but it's quite true to say that he is not a Tory. This was indirectly explained by a friend of the Prime Minister's who once said, 'To get the point of Tony you've got to understand he's really an Aussie.' What that means is that Blair has an antipodean aversion to flummery and deference, but none of the redeeming merits of Toryism: a respect for tradition, a sense of history, a reverence for custom. And that throwaway line explains something else. Blair is really an Aussie – and so is Rupert Murdoch. This is why there is a deeper bond between the two men than mere opportunism or shared interest. Murdoch shows that it possible to combine an active contempt for every form of prescriptive tradition, from the monarchy to parliamentary government, with an uncritical adoration of capitalism and its bounty.

Throughout his career Blair has shown a disdain for all

institutions, for what Bagehot called the English Constitution and not least 'the Crown in Parliament'. A small example is the way he causes much offence at Clarence House because he can't bring himself to begin letters to the Prince of Wales in the correct form, 'Sir', but has to write 'Dear Prince Charles', but that is all of a piece with the sham equalitarianism which goes hand in hand with his wealth-worship.

Although he has created more peers than any other Prime Minister, he says he has no wish to go to the House of Lords himself, since 'it's not my style'. But then the Commons has never been his style either, as he has shown by spending far less time in the chamber than any Prime Minister before. Money is his style, and that fact was to have very grave repercussions for his country. It was Peter Mandelson, Blair's *consigliere*, who wondrously pronounced that 'New Labour is intensely relaxed about people getting filthy rich', but the *capo di tutti capi* agreed. 'Britain needs more successful people who can become rich by success through the money they earn,' said Blair, and maybe Murdoch would be the man to help him become one of those successful people.

During his years as opposition leader, the most eloquent of all Blair's gestures was his journey to Australia to pay homage to Murdoch, a calculated insult to Labour to test how much they would take from their young leader. What Blair said was most revealing:

> During the sixties and seventies the left developed, almost in substitution for its economic prescriptions, which by then were failing, a type of social

individualism that confused, at points at least, liberation from prejudice with a disregard for moral structures . . . There was a real danger, occasionally realised, that single-issue pressure groups moved into the vacuum . . . I remember a telling intervention of a speaker at the Republican Convention of 1984 in the US asking rhetorically, 'When was the last time you heard a Democrat say *no*?' It was too close to the truth for comfort.

And when was the last time you heard a Labour leader quoting Republicans with approval?

But much more interesting than what Blair said was where he said it. His helping hand for Murdoch was the beginning of a fruitful association, which would see the *Sun* support Blair through three elections and act as chief drummer for his Iraq war. Murdoch himself thought the invasion would be hugely beneficial: 'The greatest thing to come out of this for the world economy, if you could put it that way, would be $20 a barrel for oil,' a misapprehension as it proved. But who knows, that friendship might yet prove the greatest thing for Tony Blair in person.

I only know what I believe

Moral chaos

When an interviewer once asked the Prime Minister about religion, Blair's sinister and shady press officer, Alastair

Campbell, was standing nearby and snapped, 'We don't do God.' But 'we' do. As Blair himself has said, religion is central to him, and his particular religious conviction explains his capacity for doing anything he wants, good or bad. He thinks he is strengthened by his faith when in fact he is undone by it. In a splendid phrase, Albert Camus said, 'If there were a party for those who weren't sure they were right, I'd belong to it.' Blair is the general secretary of the Party of Those Who Think They Are Right.

His religious faith makes him a real oddity in British politics, where it has been shared by few other Prime Ministers in the past century, and it also explains his absolute confidence in his opinions. Although he has never quite claimed that his actions were guided by prayer, he has said that 'God will be my judge'. Or, as he once all too revealingly said, 'I only know what I believe.' This confusion of empirical knowledge and irrational belief ends up with a complete disregard for truth.

By the twentieth century England had ceased to be a Christian country in any serious sense, and only a minority of prime ministers since Victoria have been Christians with a personal religion. They included Salisbury, Baldwin and Macmillan, but that characteristic Victorian agnostic Churchill was among the majority of unbelievers. That helps to distinguish this country not only from continental Europe, with its Christian Democratic parties, but from the United States, where Democrats and Republicans alike wear their religion on their sleeves, and where it's impossible to imagine a politician like Norman Tebbit, a tough, capable, populist right-winger who is also a self-proclaimed atheist. Blair has plausibly been called a Christian Democrat and in many ways he belongs to American politics more than British.

Not only is Blair unusual among politicians, so he is among his contemporaries who grew up in the 1960s and 1970s. At Oxford he met an Australian clergyman called Peter Thomson who introduced him to another writer. 'If you really want to understand what I'm all about, you have to take a look at a guy called John Macmurray,' Blair has said. 'It's all there.' Macmurray was an academic theologian and philosopher who died aged eighty-five in 1976. Blair learned from him, he says, that individuals prosper in strong, supportive communities, although like most of Blair's supposed insights this seems a vapid statement of the obvious, as are those made by his admirers. 'He holds to a set of values,' one of them has said, 'fairness, tolerance, decency,' distinguishing him from the rest of us who are passionately attached to unfairness, intolerance and indecency.

Few now read Macmurray, but in the 1930s he showed more than a passing sympathy for Marxism and other totalitarianisms. Orwell was repelled by Macmurray, calling him a 'decayed liberal' who 'can accept Russian Communism almost without reservations', though on another occasion he also wrote that 'Macmurray is saying that Hitler is right'. Macmurray's loyalties were certainly confused, until later in life when he was attracted to the Quakers and their pacifism, although this doesn't seem to have affected his most famous disciple, whom no one could accuse of pacifist sympathies.

In 1995 Blair said, 'My Christianity and my politics

came together at the same time,' and the following year he wrote an Easter essay in which he said the Tories 'have too selfish a definition of self-interest' and 'fail to look beyond, to the community'. A Whitehall joke early in Blair's prime ministerial career went that the Downing Street answering machine asked callers to 'leave a message after the high moral tone', but the moral tone became less and less convincing as the man who displayed it behaved more and more unscrupulously. Blair will very likely become a Roman Catholic after he leaves office: for years he has gone to Mass with his Catholic wife Cherie and he used to take communion, irregularly and sacrilegiously in the eyes of Catholic authority. When he was rebuked by Cardinal Hume, Blair replied 'What would Jesus have thought?' What He would indeed have thought, about everything from Ecclestone to Iraq, is a theological question still unanswered.

Whatever the basis of Blair's personal faith, the consequence of this devotion has been paradoxical. Blair evinces moral earnestness in theory, and displays a tendency to exceptionally amoral behaviour in practice. 'Far from lacking conviction, he has almost too much,' Roy Jenkins said not long before he died, with a touch of genial patronage. 'He is a little too Manichean for my perhaps now jaded taste, seeing matters in stark terms of good and evil, black and white.' That can sometimes seem so, when Blair fails to understand the truth that *le mieux est l'ennemi du bien*, that life is not a struggle between good and evil but a choice between better and worse or, in politics, as Aron said, between the preferable and the detestable.

But Blair is not only Manichean, he is antinomian: he

believes that 'to the pure all things are pure', like those heretics who thought that, if you were of the elect, you could eat, drink and merrily fornicate in the certainty of salvation. Blair is like that – not in the eating and so forth, but in his belief that his inner virtue justifies any means whatever that he chooses to employ. Before his first election he made the very foolish promise that New Labour in office would be 'purer than pure'; it may not have been an accident that, under this pious God-botherer, his government and party have acted more sordidly and corruptly than any for generations.

Among his predecessors, Gladstone was likewise sustained by the belief that his decisions were divinely inspired, or at least divinely judged. Henry Labouchere's saying that he didn't mind that the Grand Old Man always had the ace of trumps up his sleeve, only to his insisting that the Almighty had put it there, applies very well to Blair. At the end of his much more extraordinary and fruitful career, Gladstone sententiously consoled himself with the thought 'but One ever sitteth above', and Blair has said that he too will be judged by that One.

Here is the paradox. During the *Kulturkampf*, the campaign waged in the newly united German Reich against the Roman Catholic Church and the Centre, the Catholic confessional party, the formidable Bismarck found himself regularly outwitted by Centre politicians. But then, as A. J. P. Taylor observes, even Bismarck, with all his ruthlessness, 'could not rival the freedom from the principles and scruples of this world which is given by devotion to a supernatural cause'. That describes Blair exactly.

If you are convinced of your own ultimate virtue you

can do what you like – and deal with whom you want. Blair could persuade himself that it was virtuous and proper to give unconditional support to Bill Clinton at one moment and to George Bush at the next, without ever stopping to ask whether there was any contradiction, to anathematise terrorism while shaking hands with Colonel Gaddafi and Gerry Adams. More startling cases were closer at hand. Richard Desmond is the entrepreneur who now owns the *Daily Express*, but his fortune originally comes from television channels and magazines whose character can be judged from titles such as *Asian Babes*, *Skinny and Wriggly*, *The Best of Mega Boobs* and *Mothers-in-Law* (really).

A former editor of *Asian Babes* says that it was 'a strategic and conscious exercise in niche marketing', aimed at white males between thirty and fifty, although publishing it had had been 'a continually recurring nightmare' because 'Asian families have very strong cultural and religious beliefs which stress the importance of the family unit', and this had meant a shortage of available models, until ways had been found of enticing them. Blair is a doting father and a devout Christian with his own very strong cultural and religious beliefs, who used to keep a file of cuttings labelled 'Moral chaos'. The fact that he has entertained Desmond at Downing Street is an extreme case of 'to the pure all things are pure'.

This has developed into a form of almost compulsive selective amnesia, when Blair says things that are not only untrue but that a moment's conscious reflection would show could not be true. It may be a myth that he claimed to have seen Jackie Milburn play for Newcastle (which could only have been so if the infant Tony had been taken to St James's Park in nappies), but he did tell a story about being a stowaway as a young boy, for which there is no evidence. Even those fibs could have been overlooked, at least the Milburn one by sporting romantics; some of us will very likely end up telling our grandchildren that we saw Bradman play, or Hobbs.

But there was one other extraordinary moment in the summer of 1999, when Blair told a television interviewer that 'people like myself voted in favour banning fox-hunting. I voted for it.' The rights and wrongs of that question weren't the point: at the moment he said that, the Prime Minister – or rather A. C. L. Blair, the member for Sedgefield – had never once voted on any hunting Bill in the Commons, one way or the other. This was not a trivial or venial slip at all. For any legislator there could be nothing more important than what legislation he had voted on and in what sense. A man who could say that could say anything. He might even be capable of giving grossly exaggerated and distorted reasons for entering a needless war.

Magnificent lie

When fox-hunters marched through the streets of London they held placards reading 'BLIAR', and at a Labour conference left-wing protesters against the Iraq war wore the same slogan on tee-shirts, but that play on his name isn't quite accurate. 'My Tony is not a liar,' Cherie Blair said just before his third general election (or at least that was the paraphrased headline of an excruciating interview the Blairs gave in the *Sun*), and funnily enough, she's right.

Blair isn't a liar, not in the sense that most of us are. That is, most of us have on occasion told untruths, usually to get out of trouble of some kind or another (and there is no need to go into detail), but we crucially knew what we were doing. Politicians often lie in that way. Poor John Profumo told the Commons what was really the most forgivable of lies when he said that there had been no impropriety in his relationship with Christine Keeler – as Dr Johnson said, no man is required to answer a question which should not be properly be put, and how many would care to give an absolutely veracious account of their sex-lives? – while Rufus Isaacs more gravely misinformed the Commons over his Marconi investments in a way that, while not strictly false, prompted Kipling's devastating lines about 'the truthful, well-weighed answer | That tells the blacker lie'. And Anthony Eden consciously lied about the reasons why British troops were landing at Suez in 1956, knowing perfectly well that what he was saying was false but believing that it was a justifiable *ruse de guerre*.

By contrast, Blair is something different, and far more dangerous: he is not a liar but a man with no grasp at all of the distinction between objective truth and falsehood. The more sincere and intense his expression the more likely he is to be saying something that is not the case. And what makes it much worse is that, as Paddy Ashdown said ruefully and from bitter experience, 'he always means it at the time'.

By now most people recognise this and are inured to Blair's waywardness with fact, but that gift for selective amnesia remains astonishing: he will say things that are obviously and demonstrably untrue while instinctively, and too often correctly, assuming that he will not be caught out. And he often has not been, but not always. He may have given new meaning to the phrase 'getting away with murder', but now and again he is dramatically tripped up.

More than any other Prime Minister, Blair has slighted and neutered Parliament, which has forgotten its traditional role of interrogating ministers and holding the executive to account, while MPs devote themselves instead to ingratiating themselves with their constituents and collecting their enormous expenses. But occasionally there are flashes of that true purpose, when a backbencher has exposed Blair's almost psychopathic capacity for making wilfully misleading statements and for forgetting what he had already said.

Treaties of the European Union, and of course a proposed new European constitution, have to be ratified in each member state, whether by parliamentary vote or popular referendum. When the new constitution was being prepared, British Europhobes demanded a referendum, which they assumed would go against it (as referendums elsewhere had failed to pass, on the Maastricht treaty in Denmark, and the Nice treaty in Ireland, before the respective electorates were told, in the best spirit of modern European democracy, to go back and vote again until they got it right). Europhiles were correspondingly hostile to a referendum, the more so when the Murdoch press began to beat the drum for one.

As late as the autumn of 2003, Blair was still telling

friends in private that he hoped to hold and win a referendum on joining the single European currency before the next election. Even close observers of politics may be incredulous at that last sentence, but it's quite true, and it gives some indication of how detached from reality Blair had by then become. On the other hand he gave his colleagues to understand that he would not hold a referendum on the European constitution – until in 2004 he returned from sojourning in Bermuda to announce a ludicrous volte-face: there would be a referendum after all. There is every reason to suppose that this was a private deal with Rupert Murdoch, to secure his papers' support at the coming election. Blair is supposed to have told one sidekick at the time, 'I'm going to have a lot of shit to eat,' though that was as nothing compared with what he was inflicting on his party, a veritable coprophagic banquet or diet of dung, all because of his inability to hew to a straight course and tell the truth.

In the spring of 2005 the British general election was followed coincidentally by the referendums in France and the Netherlands on the constitution, with a British referendum looming as a difficult, not to say intolerable, prospect for Blair. But he was saved by the bell, or rather by the French and Dutch voters, who in both countries – to the horror of their governments, and despite the best efforts of what the contrarian French politician Jean-Pierre Chevènement accurately described as 'the soi-disant elites' – voted no.

On 5 June Blair told the Commons that, after the French and Dutch votes, 'there is no point in having a referendum, because of the uncertainty it would produce'.

At that point Angela Browning, a Tory backbencher, rose to remind Blair of what he had told the *Sun* in an interview on 13 May: 'Even if the French voted no, we would have a referendum. That is a government promise.' So it was, one of his very own. In the space of little more than three weeks he had deleted those words from his personal hard drive.

That was an almost trivial matter compared with Iraq, where one earlier exchange gave a still more frightening glimpse into Blair's mind. The most disgraceful of all arguments used by proponents of the war – once it became clear that the original justifications had collapsed – was to say that critics of the invasion didn't want Iraq to become a democracy and didn't care about Saddam's tyranny. When Kenneth Clarke, standing yet again without success for the Tory leadership in 2005, understandably reminded people that he had warned beforehand what folly the war would be, Matthew d'Ancona wrote sarcastically, 'It is nice for Mr Clarke that he feels so triumphantly vindicated. It would be even nicer if he had had the grace to say that Saddam's removal was welcome,' to which Clarke might have replied that it would be nicer still if people like d'Ancona could remember that 'Saddam's removal' was specifically not the reason why we were meant to have gone to war.

Needless to say, no one used this line more shamelessly than Blair. In the Commons on 13 October 2004, he abused Charles Kennedy, the Liberal Democrat leader, who had opposed the war, saying that if Kennedy had had his way, 'Saddam Hussein and his sons would still be running Iraq. And that is why I took the stand I did. I take it now and I at least will stick by it.' This time it was a Labour backbencher, Bob Wareing, who rose to ask how, in view of what he just said, Blair could 'explain his statement to this House on 25 February 2003 when he said, "Even now, today, we are offering Saddam the prospect of voluntarily disarming through the United Nations. I detest his regime but even now he could save it by complying with the United Nations' demands."'

On both occasions Blair was speechless, with no possible reply. But then he doesn't need to justify what he has said or explain any contradiction in his statements, however blatant or grotesque. Whatever happens, however much goes wrong, however many times he is detected in falsehood, he obliterates it in his own mind. In his own favourite phrases, it's time to draw a line and move on.

To this day the settlement in Northern Ireland is widely, though not universally, regarded as one of Blair's true achievements. Whether that is the case, what the former Irish Prime Minister John Bruton, in a moment of eloquent exasperation, called 'the fucking peace process' showed some of Blair's worst failings on the way. First of all there was the unconsciously risible rhetoric, when he arrived in Belfast in Holy Week of 1998 to say, with his most pious and sincere expression, although with no sense of the ludicrous as he barely paused between two sentences, 'This is no time for soundbites. I feel the hand of history on our shoulders.' Maybe there were people who actually impressed by that, but it got worse. As Simon Jenkins has correctly observed, Blair may be a good performer but he is a very bad negotiator. While strutting the stage and striking attitudes and talking about the hand of history, he has again and again been outplayed, in his dealings with European heads of governments or with American presidents. He has again and again given, and got nothing in return. Never was that more true than in the Northern Ireland negotiations, when Gerry Adams ran rings round him.

In any case, the whole 'peace process' was inherently mendacious, which may be why it suited Blair so well. A complacent phrase came to be used by officials about the 'constructive ambiguity' on which the process was based, meaning that each side could understand any part of the agreement to mean what they wanted it to mean, made worse by Blair and his personal propensity to misrepresent the situation to both parties. One *Irish Times* columnist went further, writing about the 'magnificent lie' on which the process rested. When that cynical eighteenth-century politico Lord Holland heard some piece of public chicanery described as a pious fraud, he said, 'I see the fraud, but where is the piety?' and in Ulster it was easier to see the lie than the magnificence.

Even after the agreement was drawn up and agreed by the different parties, the obvious ambiguity remained. The agreement had to be endorsed by referendum in both parts of Ireland. One meeting was held at Ballymoney, a Protestant village in County Antrim, where the case for voting yes was made by David Trimble, the Unionist leader, Kate Hoey – herself an Ulsterwoman – for the government and Lord Cranborne for the Tory opposition. I well remember covering that meeting, and how the Unionist leader was discomposed when an intelligent schoolboy asked him, 'Mr Trimble, you say you are recommending your followers to vote yes because it will strengthen Northern Ireland's place in the Union. Gerry Adams says he is recommending his followers to vote yes because it will lead to a united Ireland. Can you both be right?'

Because most Unionists were so suspicious about the agreement, which seemed to them, not surprisingly, a capitulation to the IRA, Trimble needed help. And so on top of the text of the agreement itself, Blair provided a number of 'side' promises, the most important of which was 'no prisoner releases unless violence ended for good'. Whether constructive or not, that was unambiguous; it was scarcely magnificent, but it was a lie: republican as well as loyalist terrorist murderers were released from prison, and violence continued for years. It was a promise Blair had made with no intention of keeping.

That lie ended Trimble's career, which meant that the outcome was very much not as Blair had hoped. He had wanted to see devolved government in the province, with Trimble and nationalists sharing power. But Trimble was destroyed politically by Blair's duplicity. Within a matter of years his Ulster Unionists had collapsed electorally, trounced and replaced by the Democratic Unionists. In this way, Trimble joined a long line of victims.

When a political leader gives someone else to understand something and then quite forgets what was understood between them, then that other is, in the hallowed phrase of Irish politics, left with his arse hanging out of the window. The line began with Gordon Brown, who must have expected, after their deal at Granita in 1994, to have succeeded Blair before 2007, and who was

these excruciating verbless sentences and said, 'New Labour. New Government. New Red Boxes. New Cars. New Salaries.' That is why his career as Labour leader was an exercise in bad faith from the beginning. It had to be. Blair was always trying to say too many things to too many different people, to square circles and reconcile the irreconcilable. And Blair could never quite carry off his attempts to justify this, because he had a superficial eloquence but little deep mental capacity.

Despite his disappointment, Roy Jenkins continued to admire Blair, and there was on the face of it much in common between what the defectors who formed the Social Democratic Party in 1982 had hoped to do to Labour and what Blair had apparently succeeded in doing. But Jenkins had described Blair in his splendidly *de haut en bas* way as 'a second-rate intellect but a first-rate temperament'; he contrasted him with Brown, who was the other way round, and suggested that the Blair combination was the better suited to politics. It's true that the last British Prime Minister who could be called an intellectual was Sir Anthony Eden (although aesthete might be a better word), and look what happened to him.

Others have pitched it lower than second class. After the eccentric pop singer George Michael had dined with the Blairs he said that Blair 'didn't seem the brightest guy in the room'. Barbara Cassani, the American who at one time led the British bid to stage the 2012 Olympics in London also dined with Blair. 'To be frank', she thought that 'he wasn't that bright'. As she well put it, he 'has this ability to make it seem as if he cares, but he didn't seem particularly knowledgeable about anything'. And the

44

novelist Doris Lessing puts it better still: 'He believes in magic. That if you say a thing, it is true. I think he's not very bright in some ways.' Blair himself almost admits this: 'When I was young, I paid more regard to intellect than judgement. As I've got older, I pay more regard to judgement than to intellect,' which sounds nice in a homespun way until you wonder what the distinction between judgement and intellect really is, and for that matter how well he scores on either.

His problem isn't so much what a don might call his beta brain as his ignorance, lack of intellectual curiosity and absence of any broader general culture. As Paul Johnson, another friend and admirer, has ruefully admitted, 'he never reads a book', and it shows. 'Never' is not literally true: Blair claims to have read the Koran no fewer than three times (although we don't know whether he drew Cherie's attention to the thirty-fourth verse of the fourth chapter, *An-Nisa*, 'The Women', which says that husbands with troublesome wives should 'admonish them and leave them alone in the sleeping-places and beat them').

Otherwise Blair is, for someone who has, in the old phrase, enjoyed a long and expensive education, remarkably uncultivated and ill read. Not only does he have no serious interest in art or music; when on different occasions he was asked for his favourite poem and favourite novel, and with the fathomless riches of English literature to choose from, he could do no better than name Rupert Brooke's 'The Soldier' ('If I should die, think only this of me . . .') and *Ivanhoe*, which may be the worst novel Sir Walter Scott ever wrote. Even that would matter less than the ignorance of history he has so often betrayed, and which has revealed itself all too painfully. If he had read less of the Koran and more about the making of the modern Middle East he might have acted more wisely than he has.

Because Blair has an instinctive and not a reflective mind, his attempts to give any theoretical substance to his politics were always embarrassing. So were all the supposed exegeses of New Labour and the Third Way. It were kinder to pass over the vapourings of Anthony (now of course Lord) Giddens, who became one of the alleged intellectual commissars of the party, and also the sorry agitprop which appeared as *The Blair Revolution* by Peter Mandelson and *The Unfinished Revolution: How the Modernisers Saved the Labour Party* by Philip Gould, whose writers could at least be excused as singing for their suppers.

A more comical case was Will Hutton, the stockbroker turned journalist who had written *The State We're In*, a best-selling book on the woes endured under the Tories. In 1997 he published *The State to Come*, a flag-waving tract which came out just before the election proclaiming that 'only a future Labour government will be able to set a new agenda for Britain'. These were revolutionary times, Blair was a great radical reforming leader who would transform the country, we were witnessing 'the strange rebirth of liberal England', a Blair government would raise income tax, redistribute wealth, strengthen the trade unions. Above all, Hutton insisted that the Blairite state to come would immediately seek to join the single European currency.

Ten years on it is effortless to mock prophecies almost

entirely falsified by events, but the veteran journalist Robert Taylor did so at the time, making mincemeat of Hutton and his teenybopper optimism. There was no chance whatever that we were about to see a great new progressive era comparable with those which began with the elections in 1868 or 1906 or 1945, Taylor wrote. How Labour's smart young spin-doctors in Millbank Tower must have been laughing at Hutton's absurdities. They knew from their own polling and focus groups that what Middle England wanted was market economics powdered with caring rhetoric. 'The New Labour "project" looks increasingly like Margaret Thatcher's final triumph,' Taylor said with genuine prescience.

Although Hutton insisted awkwardly that New Labour 'is not a completely empty political vessel', it was significant that he addressed that as a possibility. Others at the time saw that Blair was really engaged less in a political revolution than in a marketing exercise for 'Labour Lite'. His first election was covered for the *New Yorker* by Joe Klein, the 'Anonymous' author of *Primary Colors*, who saw Blair as a pop-toaster salesman, whatever that might be, and said that the closer you looked at New Labour the more it seemed a clever rhetorical device whose purpose was to reassure a group of technocrats that they had not after all became middle-aged conservatives.

As if nervous about such accusations, in 1998 Blair attempted his own doctrinal justification, in a pamphlet called *The Third Way: New Politics for a New Century*. It was published in the week that he also discussed the subject at a meeting with Bill Clinton, who by unhappy timing had just given new meaning to the phrase 'third way' by his dealings with Monica Lewinsky, but when the sniggering had died down plucky readers could tackle a pamphlet which began, 'I have always believed that politics is first and foremost about ideas.'

Apart from their leaden banality, those words were of course quite untrue. So the rest of the pamphlet showed, but it was revealing for all that. 'My vision for the twenty-first century is of a populist politics reconciling themes which in the past have wrongly been regarded as antagonistic – patriotism *and* internationalism, rights *and* responsibilities; the promotion of enterprise *and* the attack on poverty and discrimination.' The moment a reader blinked, it was obvious that these weren't antagonistic at all, and that the list was merely platitudinous. What politician opposes enterprise *and* favours poverty?

Just as Blair thought he had said something original when he talked about the end of ideology, he now preened himself as he defined a principle of 'permanent revisionism'. This meant 'a continual search for better means to meet our goals', for which 'a large measure of pragmatism is essential'. To the limited extent that any sense could be extracted from this verbiage, it was that he could do exactly as he liked at any moment, that words meant what he chose them to mean, that the Third Way was whatever he chose to do at any moment, and that whatever he did was good. A natural if sometimes morbid concern with communication had turned into its own justification. The means became the ends, the medium the message; as Wagner unkindly said of Meyerbeer's music, Blairism is all effects and no causes. Truly, 'New Labour is the new politics'.

48

Third Way, New Order

Like a bride's outfit, Blair's rhetoric was something old, something new, something borrowed and something blue. The blue was the purloining of rhetoric, and for that matter policies, from the Conservatives. The borrowing was Blair's equally adroit use of the language of 'stake-holding' popularised by Hutton. 'We need to build a relationship of trust not just within a firm but within a society,' Blair told a meeting of businessmen in Singapore in January 1996. 'By trust, I mean the recognition of a mutual purpose for which we work together and in which we all benefit. It is a stakeholder economy, in which opportunity is available to all, advancement is through merit, and from which no group or class is set apart or excluded.' This was the language of the 'big tent', which reached its sublimely absurd apotheosis on the night of the 2001 election, when the Tory defector Shaun Woodward said that New Labour was 'a party for everyone, not of any particular class or any particular view'.

Something new is one way of describing the execrable jargon which made Blair and his party a laughing stock: 'blue sky thinking', 'paradigm shift', 'roll out', 'front-loading', 'progressive universalism', 'step change' and 'joined-up government'. But if that was comical, the something old was much more frightening.

Before he was elected, Blair said that New Labour was 'the political wing of the British people', and on election day in 1997 he boasted, 'We have won support from all walks of life, all classes of people. We are now today the people's party, the party of all the people.' Another leader had once spoken in strikingly similar terms. 'To be national can only mean to be behind your people, and to be socialist can only be to stand up for the right of your people . . . Not purely nationalist or socialist, bourgeois or proletarian,' Hitler said. 'The party is a movement which is . . . toiling and working for the existence of the people.'

Although Blair is not a totalitarian, it is notorious that some of the most ardent supporters he acquired, political and journalistic, were former communists and Trotskyists, attracted by ruthlessness and lack of principle for their own sake. John Reid is perhaps the most striking member of the Cabinet, relishing his own brutality while he outlines another outrageous assault on individual freedom in the quiet tones his fellow communists used to call 'patiently explaining'.

While Blair is not a fascist himself any more than a communist, he and his party have continually if unconsciously echoed the language of fascism, to a degree which shows a truly astonishing tone-deafness to twentieth-century history. Even before he became Prime Minister, Blair spoke in one of his most extravagant rhetorical flights of 'a thousand days to prepare for a thousand years'. Could he really have forgotten who had once promised a Thousand-Year Reich? Although 'New Labour' was never formally adopted as the party's name, Blair never lost an opportunity to use the phrase: when he became prime minister he relentlessly hammered away at the word 'New', once again forgetting who had ruled a *Neue Ordnung* or New Order sixty years before.

It is quite wrong to see the integral-nationalist or fascist movements of the first half of the century as conservative.

'Newness' and modernity were the rhetorical stock in trade of fascism, and new meant young. Soon after Blair came to power a video called *Young Country* was inflicted on the Commonwealth leaders when they came to a meeting in what used, much more accurately, to be called the old country. England is indeed remarkably old, older than almost any in Europe in terms of history and national consciousness, and it is nowadays a notably old country as to demographic profile also. No government, including Blair's, has begun seriously to address the implications of this ageing of society, in which life expectancy increases year by year so that the ratio of the productive working population to the retired shrinks drastically. But in any case the leader – or Duce – of the New Order – or New Labour – had forgotten that there was once another party whose marching song was called 'Youth'. It was Mussolini's Fascists who sang 'Giovinezza': 'Youth, youth, springtime of beauty . . .'.

Another favourite New Labour word was 'people's'. Blair led the way with 'we are now today the people's party', one minister boasted about the 'people's opera', another spoke of the 'people's Wimbledon', and most famously – if fatuously – of all, on the morrow of Princess Diana's death Blair said that she was 'a people's princess', a phrase handed him by Alastair Campbell at his most cynical and foolish. It remains an entirely preposterous description of that poor little rich girl.

In any case Blair and his colleagues had once again forgotten about the 'people's car' – the Volkswagen, beloved of Hitler – or the People's Police – the Vopos, who once maintained order in the German Democratic

Republic. Both Soviet Socialist Russia and National Socialist Germany had people's courts, a name which Blair has yet to borrow, though that may have been an oversight.

Thanks to his invincible historical ignorance, Blair never stopped to think about those words, or to ask why 'modernising' – that other key word in the New Labour vocabulary – was so obviously desirable. Early in the twentieth century, modernity was often connected with a broader reaction against the rational, a tendency which was so important in political and cultural life. This produced ultra-nationalism, bolshevism, and fascism, not to say the Great War itself.

After Mussolini came Hitler, and a Third Reich which has been acutely described by the American historian John Lukacs in words which, if one didn't know the context, might read like a description of New Labour: 'It was democratic; and it was modern . . . in almost every sense of the word anti-traditionalist.' The English travel writer Robert Byron visited Germany in 1938 and watched the Nuremberg rally, where he was struck precisely by its modernity: 'The whole ceremonial is of a remarkable kind . . . and it is new in that it incorporates, indeed is based on, the last resources of the age.'

Even the beloved 'Third Way' displayed a painful ignorance of the past. In 1923, the German rightist Arthur Moeller van den Bruck wrote a book commending a new order of national zeal and discipline, which would, as it proved, be born less than ten years later. He called this book *Das dritte Reich*, the Third Reich, a name Hitler would appropriate, but the writer only thought of that at the last moment. Almost until the book went to press, it was to be called *Der dritte Weg* – The Third Way. That phrase would often be used between the wars by other fascists. On the one side was corrupt liberal democracy, on the other was communism: fascism offered a Third Way between them.

Over the years Blair won cheers and ovations with his party conference speeches. Each one deserves close textual analysis, none more so than the 1999 speech in which he denounced the 'forces of conservatism' and – in that phrase already used in the 1997 manifesto – called New Labour the 'political wing of the British people'. Two years later, in the wake of 11 September, he gave his most exalted oration of all, in which he had his deluded followers quivering orgasmically when he said, 'The starving, the wretched, the dispossessed, the ignorant, those living in want and squalor, from the deserts of northern Africa to the slums of Gaza, to the mountain ranges of Afghanistan: they too are our cause . . . The kaleidoscope has been shaken. The pieces are in flux. Soon they will settle again. Before they do, let us reorder this world around us.'

Some observers date their doubts about the man's sanity from that moment. The reference to the slums of Gaza was merely demagogic and hypocritical: Blair was already acting as Washington's global cheerleader, as well as what one American writer accurately called 'Bush's ambassador to America', and there was nothing whatever he was likely to do for the Palestinians except exploit them for rhetorical effect. But the peroration was not merely high flown, it was deranged. When the man next to you in the pub starts talking about the pieces of the kaleidoscope in flux, you make an excuse and leave quickly, before he goes on to explain the meaning of life in terms of the dimensions of the Great Pyramid.

As to the 'forces of conservatism' speech, some years later Richard Jenkyns, the Oxford classicist and literary critic, wrote an essay on politics and language – Orwell's great subject – in *Prospect*, in which he looked hard at it and, in all seriousness, called it the most fascistic speech ever given by a leading British politician. It soon turned out that what Blair meant by those forces of conservatism comprised honourable Tories, principled socialists, honest radicals, old-fashioned liberals: in fact anyone at all who happened not to agree with him. New Labour was a party for everyone; it was a big tent which would include all the good people, what was known in 1930s Germany as *Gleichschaltung* or assimilation, and that in turn meant that anyone not included was by definition bad. Such demonisation of all other political forces had been a stock in trade of fascism: they were not merely one's opponents, as in constitutional democracies, they were the enemy.

Even more telling was that repeated phrase 'the political wing of the British people'. This was a play on the old terminology in which there was a Labour movement, whose industrial wing was the unions and whose political wing was the Labour Party. But fascist leaders always claimed that they alone represented the people: if one party is the political voice of the whole nation, then what need is there of any other parties?

No amount of derision could halt the flood of New Labour jargon and verbiage. Even in November 2006

Ruth Kelly was still addressing the Commons in fluent Blair-speak: 'Sustained investment, not short-termism or cuts. Supporting aspiration for everyone, not privilege for a few.' And yet it was not merely laughable. As Orwell might have said, New Labour spoke a language in which it was impossible to tell the truth – but in which it was certainly possible to tell untruths.

It would not be long before the master himself began to 'reconcile more antagonistic themes', by telling Parliament and people that he was doing everything he could to work for peace, while telling the American President that he would do everything he could to support his war. 'When I use a word, it means just what I choose it to mean – neither more nor less,' said Humpty Dumpty, and no one understood that better than Blair.

Prime Minister of the United States

A just war

It has been – or it was – a proud boast by George W. Bush that he was 'a war President'. However that unhappy phrase might now seem in his case, Blair is most certainly a war Prime Minister. His zeal for waging war was quite unforeseen ten years ago but it is by this that he will be remembered.

In the very month he became Prime Minister he said that 'ours is the first generation able to contemplate that we may live our entire lives without going to war or sending our children to war', not words that are now likely to appear as his epitaph.

Although many of the crimes and follies of his career were adumbrated in his character and conduct from an early stage, it would have been difficult until he became Prime Minister to discern his belief that he was a new Churchill, or that he had a mission to right the wrongs of the whole world. There was a universal assumption before Blair reached Downing Street that his government would be judged by success or failure in domestic politics, and that any verdict on his career would depend on the economy, health and education, crime and poverty. The only 'foreign' issue which seemed central and pressing was relations with Europe in general and British membership of the single currency in particular, which his deluded admirers insisted would define his premiership.

But then running a country is a difficult and messy business, especially in a parliamentary democracy, however attenuated. All the fatuous jargon about targets and joined-up government and 'what works' ran up against sticky reality, and the fundamental conflict between Blair and his party, inert and supine as it had become.

Making war was different. Some corner of a foreign field could be forever Tony, at least in spirit. He could strike attitudes, throw around the thunderbolts of rhetoric, win the plaudits of well-meaning Americans, play the he-man. Robin Cook saw this. He resigned from the government when the Iraq war began, but otherwise remained loyal in public to Blair. In private he lamented that his old colleague had been carried away by the thrill of power. Blair was excited, he was exalted – and in the end he was undone – by the big wars that make ambition virtue.

No other Prime Minister has waged so many wars; and this appetite grows with the eating. He managed to get through 1997 without sending British soldiers to kill and be killed, and the first two of 'his' wars in 1998 were barely wars at all. British forces were in action in the Sierra Leone escapade and in Operation Desert Fox (it was said that the codenames of military operations in the Second World War, Overlord or Anvil, betrayed Churchill's literary tastes; the names of some recent Israeli and American–British operations, Peace in Galilee or Iraqi Freedom, may seem more redolent of Orwell). In the former, the Foreign Office first of all carelessly allowed the supply of arms and mercenaries to a temporarily destabilised government in Sierra Leone, and then begged for a scratch 'special battalion' of British troops to help evacuate foreign nationals and to clear up a little of the mess; in the latter a few RAF Tornados helped a much larger American bombing operation against 250 targets in Iraq.

One of the few creditable things about Bill Clinton was his disinclination to send American forces into action, recognising that as a former draft-dodger it became him to show restraint, a contrast indeed to his chicken-hawk successor, and also to his new friend Blair. Clinton had suffered a nervous shock, as had the American people, with the Somali debacle in 1993, when a handful of American special forces died unpleasant and dramatic deaths. The Americans forgot about the 500 Somalis who died on that day and remembered only the eighteen Americans whose bodies were dragged through the streets of Mogadishu. And so the following year when an old festering conflict between two peoples in Rwanda erupted into appalling bloodshed, Clinton did nothing. Many people were left with a bad conscience, not least Clinton, who later gave one of his more egregious performances of sickly penitence.

All the same, his administration had devised a Presidential Decision Directive listing sixteen factors which had to be considered before American troops were committed to peacekeeping missions. These criteria were almost deliberately designed not to be met; or as one Congressman said with approval, the list ensured 'zero degree of involvement and zero degree of risk and zero degree of pain and confusion'.

In the summer of 1998 Clinton ordered the bombing of Sudan, so that a legitimate pharmaceutical factory was destroyed and innocent life lost, but this was just a stunt to distract attention from his undignified domestic travails. So was Desert Fox, the bombing of Iraq. It said still more about Blair's amorality underlying his public piety that he could present himself as a friend and ally of someone like Clinton and act as a human shield for the President during those travails, even if it meant the killing of more innocents. As it happened, and by a great irony, Desert Fox may actually have succeeded in military terms. It reinforced what the first Gulf war had accomplished, checking any ambitions Saddam may have nurtured to develop 'weapons of mass destruction' and making unnecessary any invasion of Iraq.

By contrast, in Kosovo, Afghanistan and the invasion of Iraq, Blair really could claim real credit, if that was the word. The first of those was very much 'his war', and the year 1999 was crucial in several ways: Blair was waging war as never before, he advanced a theoretical justification for doing so, and he thereby quite transformed his reputation in America. Unlike Sierra Leone, the Kosovo conflict was important; unlike Desert Fox, it was Blair's own pet. He urged a reluctant Clinton to step up the campaign against Serbia. In March a NATO bombing campaign began, ostensibly with the purpose 'Serbs out, peacekeepers in, refugees back', and it continued to the end of the year, causing many civilian casualties, precipitating a flood of refugees and aggravating an incipient civil war between Serbs and Kosovars.

In May Blair went to Aix-la-Chapelle (or Aachen) to receive the Charlemagne Prize as a 'good European'. Not many years later they might have felt like asking for their prize back, but at that time his star still burned brightly in Europe as well as America. In Aix Blair reiterated that the campaign in Kosovo and Serbia must be pursued to the end, with new windy rhetoric about 'no compromises, no fudge, no half-baked ideals', once again representing himself as the most resolute leader of any NATO country, an implied contrast not least with Clinton. But that speech is much less important than one he had made shortly before in Chicago, on a sabre-rattling tour of America whose rhetorical high point this speech was.

This speech is of the first importance, not least because it won Blair huge credit among American liberals. It wasn't for another two or more years that the phrase 'Blair

Democrats' caught on, at least for a time, but in that late spring of 1999 he was hailed as 'the Prime Minister of the United States', 'Blair for President' bumper stickers appeared, Dana Milbank was moved to say in the *New Republic* that at last the United States had 'a leader who is acting presidential' on the international stage, before adding ruefully, 'Unfortunately, this leader is Tony Blair,' and Paul Berman, the political writer, said more simply that Blair was 'the leader of the free world'. These enthusiasts would have much to answer for within five years.

Even at that time his interventionist rantings were humbug, but they worked in whipping up such frenzied camp followers. Throughout the dismal years of Blair's premiership there was a comic subplot, the incurable, indefatigable capacity for delusion among his admirers on the liberal left while he played his usual devious game trying to satisfy both sides at once, left and right, 'liberal hawks' and non-interventionists. In May 1997 the *Observer* had screeched 'Goodbye to xenophobia' without quite noticing what Blair had just said about the sacred pound sterling, which he loved as much as any *Sun* reader. Now Milbank and Berman cannot have noticed what Blair had just told the same newspaper: 'I won't send our boys in.'

For all that, it was an impressive speech he gave in Chicago, not surprisingly since it was largely written by Sir Lawrence Freedman, the distinguished military historian and theorist. After the usual inane pleasantries ('there is a long British history with Chicago . . . Chicagoland is the headquarters of some of Britain's most important inward investors') which Freedman presumably didn't contribute, the Prime Minister moved on to more serious matters:

No one in the West who has seen what is happening in Kosovo can doubt that NATO's military action is justified. Bismarck famously said the Balkans were not worth the bones of one Pomeranian grenadier. Anyone who has seen the tear-stained faces of the hundreds of thousands of refugees streaming across the border, heard their heart-rending tales of cruelty or contemplated the unknown fates of those left behind knows that Bismarck was wrong.

This is a just war, based not on any territorial ambitions but on values. We cannot let the evil of ethnic cleansing stand. We must not rest until it is reversed. We have learned twice before in this century that appeasement does not work. If we let an evil dictator range unchallenged, we will have to spill infinitely more blood and treasure to stop him later.

All of that was designed to tickle the susceptibilities of all those who felt frustrated and impotent anger in the face of distant oppression, but it begged several questions. Why this was a NATO action at all, or why indeed was NATO still in existence? This is one of the unexamined mysteries of the age. For forty years after its creation in 1949, NATO fulfilled its task with brilliant success. Not only was western Europe guarded against Russian aggression, but in the end the Soviet Union itself imploded and its empire disintegrated. When the Berlin Wall fell the logical thing would have been to hold a splendid party with magnums of Bollinger and fine delicacies on the boulevard Leopold III in Brussels to mark the winding up of NATO after that mission was fully accomplished. Few of us then realised that NATO would not only remain in business but subtly change its purpose to become an instrument of American policy, while its reach would be continually expanded far beyond its original and clearly defined field of operation, now to the Gulf of Riga and the Dniester, then to the Pamirs and the Tigris, *und morgen die ganze Welt*. Even now NATO defines itself by the 1949 treaty which said that an armed attack on any member

> in Europe or North America shall be considered an attack against them all and consequently they agree that, if such an armed attack occurs, each of them, in exercise of the right of individual or collective self-defence recognised by Article 51 of the Charter of the United Nations, will assist the Party or Parties so attacked by taking forthwith, individually and in concert with the other Parties, such action as it deems necessary, including the use of armed force, to restore and maintain the security of the North Atlantic area.

By the autumn of 2006 NATO was proudly proclaiming one of its latest feats: 'Record drug seizure in Afghanistan'. No one has explained what that has to do with the original treaty, or by what geographical conjuring trick 'the North Atlantic area' has been extended to the edge of the Himalayas. But it suits Blair.

Really terrible wars

What Blair was saying was drastic in another way. He talked glibly of the end of the era which had began with the Peace of Westphalia (not 'Treaty' as he called it) recognising the sovereignty of states, all leaving each other alone and not trying to change each other's political character by force. Now things had changed. 'Many of our problems have been caused by two dangerous and ruthless men – Saddam Hussein and Slobodan Milošević. Both have been prepared to wage vicious campaigns against sections of their own community,' which was of course true, but then the same could be said of many tyrants. No one then put to Blair the obvious point: if he was going to wage war against any country ruled by brutal and bloodthirsty tyrants, then we would never know a day's peace. Was that what he wanted? Perhaps it was.

A sleight of hand was already visible: Saddam and Milošević were brutal despots, but almost without drawing breath Blair would suggest that this made them a threat to British national interests. He quoted Bismarck's derisive phrase as if the words were self-evidently those of a cynical reactionary, but Bismarck was only saying in his own way what the radical Quaker John Bright had said:

How are the interests of England involved in this question? . . . It is not on a question of sympathy that I dare involve this country, or any country, in war which must cost an incalculable amount of treasure and blood. It is not my duty to make my country the

knight-errant of the human race, and to take upon
herself the protection of the thousand millions of
human beings who have been permitted by the
Creator of all things to people this planet.

Bright was a Christian of different kind from Blair, and the
modern left were also of a different cut; they had quite
forgotten Bright's language, to the great convenience of
Blair, and before long to the calamity of his country.

Then came the nub of Blair's speech:

So how do we decide when and whether to intervene?
I think we need to bear in mind five major
considerations. First, are we sure of our case? War is
an imperfect instrument for fighting humanitarian
distress, but armed force is sometimes the only means
of dealing with dictators. Second, have we exhausted
all diplomatic options? We should always give peace
every chance, as we have in the case of Kosovo. Third,
on the basis of a practical assessment of the situation,
are there military operations we can sensibly and
prudently undertake? Fourth, are we prepared for the
long term? In the past we talked too much of exit
strategies. But having made a commitment we cannot
simply walk away once the fight is over; better to stay
with moderate numbers of troops than return for
repeat performances with large numbers. And finally,
do we have national interests involved?

Those words seem lucid and unambiguous, and I have
quoted them at some length because of their relevance to

the disastrous Iraq enterprise. We shall return to them later.

Those American admirers could not have realised how much their praise was encouraging Blair's considerable vanity. Historical circumstance had given him the opportunity not to *be* a world leader but to *play* a world leader. An American President, of either party, Clinton or Bush the Younger, might be called 'leader of the free world' by his own supporters, but the phrase would seem comical outside America. And how could any other European leader, French President or German Chancellor, plausibly assume that mantle? But Blair for the time being played the part well enough to have a large audience cheering, and himself purring with prideful pleasure. Any Prime Minister struggles at home with tedious and intractable problems. What Prime Minister, wrestling with hospitals and railways at one moment, would not be flattered and exhilarated to be told that he was the leader of the free world at the next? With one bound our hero was unchained from his cares. He wasn't any other politician, he was a Great Man.

Not every American was quite so awestruck by his grandiloquent oratory as were Milbank and Berman. The right-wing populist Patrick Buchanan observed sarcastically that that if an army were needed for this Balkan crusade it wouldn't be British troops slogging toward Belgrade, and he was absolutely right. All of Blair's interventionist bravura was fundamentally dishonest, because of the extreme disparity of the United States and the United Kingdom – or of America and Europe – in military terms. Henry Kissinger said that he would take

'Europe' seriously when it had a telephone number he could call in an international crisis; he might have added, and when Europe has forces which can match its leaders' big talk.

In that punitive 'NATO' bombing campaign against Serbia, more than three-quarters of sorties were flown by the American aircraft, and the disproportion would be even greater in Iraq, for a simple reason. For fifty years European countries have relentlessly reduced their armed forces and their military spending. As long ago as 1956 President Eisenhower anticipated Buchanan in complaining that Europeans wouldn't shoulder their share of the burden of common defence, and he would have had as much cause for complaint over the next half-century.

In 1939 the United States barely ranked as a military power, with a smaller army than Belgium, and during the frightful first half of the twentieth century with its two great wars the numbers of Americans killed, proportionately or absolutely, was trifling by European standards. After 1950 the story was quite different. The British Army and the Royal Navy were steadily run down, so that by the time Blair became Prime Minister, the British Crown had fewer men under arms than in the 1780s, at the time we were fighting the rebellious Americans. Between 1951, when Attlee left Downing Street, and 1997, when Blair arrived there, the proportion of British state spending devoted to defence fell from 24 per cent to 7 per cent; in the same period, the proportion which went on health and welfare rose from 22 per cent to 53 per cent. One of Blair's hopes when he became Prime Minister had been to curb the sprawling growth of welfare, and in that he would fail utterly. But the failure had deep implications for his grandiose foreign policy as well.

For more than half a century, with a choice between 'guns or butter', the Americans have chosen guns, and the Europeans have chosen butter. There is an exiguous American welfare state, and Europeans are continually surprised by how hard Americans work, how modest their pay often is, and how short their holidays are, by contrast with Europe's lavish welfare, high wages and creature comforts: as the Germans say, 'we have the youngest pensioners in Europe, and the oldest students, the shortest working week and the longest holidays', and that was only marginally less true of the British. And yet the hard-working American taxpayer has indirectly subsidised the European welfare stare by paying almost all the cost of common defence.

As his zeal for making war began to grow, there was not so much fantasy as a display of Blair's wonderful uncon-sciousness. Although he would have been be shocked if told that he had chosen to 'take up the White Man's burden', that is just what he did. But he had forgotten the lesson of Kipling's great poem. Before his disastrous prime ministership was finished he would know all about 'The blame of those ye better, | The hate of those ye guard', and he would have done well to remember the admonition: 'Nor call too loud on Freedom | To cloak your weariness.'

Often enough Blair has been called Margaret Thatcher's heir, but she was often wiser and more far-seeing than he. Twenty years before the invasion of Iraq she had anticipated Blair's arguments when she said that the western democracies 'use our force to preserve our way of life. We do not use it to walk into other people's countries, independent sovereign territories.' If a new law is ordained that wherever an evil regime holds sway, 'there the United States shall enter, then we are going to have really terrible wars in the world'. Never did she speak more prophetically.

In 1999, Bill Clinton was still in office, and when Blair gave his Chicago speech George Bush the Younger was still a year and three-quarters away from the White House. Nobody, including Blair himself, could possibly have foreseen the coming events, including the way the Prime Minister would act as a human shield for another President, providing rhetorical cover for a needless and illegal war, but that was always inherent. And yet Blair's language of humanitarian intervention was deeply hypocritical throughout, because he willed the ends without willing the means.

Part Two:

Washington's International Gofer

Thank you for coming

Populist values

During the 2001 general election a riveting description appeared, by a famous writer. The Prime Minister wins re-election while preaching the virtues of wealth creation and the free market. Even now, which is to say before the 11 September attacks and their sequel, he is an ardent supporter of the United States, to the point where, unlike most other European leaders, he is ready to endorse 'son of star wars', the fanciful plan for a missile shield, and any further American military enterprises as yet undreamed of.

Not everyone would be overjoyed by a fresh electoral victory. This astute literary observer is himself among the Prime Minister's sharpest critics, and critical also of the electorate, comparing their readiness to vote for him with the religious credulity of primitive tribes. But then the leader's greatest insight is to have 'understood the collapse of traditional ideology and its replacement by the populist values of the mass media'.

To anyone covering Blair's second general election those words seemed faultlessly apt. What made them so uncanny was that they weren't by any English writer at all but by Umberto Eco, describing the almost contemporaneous Italian general election in which, just before Blair, Silvio Berlusconi was returned to power.

Before then the two men had already discovered an affinity. Tony and Cherie Blair have a keen appetite for luxurious freeloading holidays abroad. They later took to staying at Sir Cliff Richard's Barbados beach house, and they found another happy berth, a princely palazzo in Tuscany with its own vineyards, olive groves and home-made delicacies. It was the kind of holiday home any member of the educated upper-middle classes would kill for, as Boris Johnson remarked, adding that we had long wondered what Blair was really for and against, but at last we knew: 'he is *pro*sciutto and *anti*pasto'.

Now the Blairs were entertained at Berlusconi's gloriously vulgar palace in Sardinia, where Blair became warm friends with this colourful plutocrat who had gained effective control over a large part of the Italian media and had concentrated more and more political power on himself with the object not least of securing immunity from investigation into his lurid business dealings. Blair has said very tellingly that 'there isn't a world of difference' politically between him and the American neoconservatives, and he might have said that there wasn't a world of difference either between his values and his friend Silvio's. He can certainly make a statement by the company he chooses.

Not that Blair's friendship is an absolute quality. He has a knack of supporting those closest to him with complete loyalty, right up to the moment when they get in his way. At the beginning of 2001 Peter Mandelson was ejected from the government for the second and last time. The proximate cause was the Hinduja affair, yet another proof, like Ecclestone before and Mittal after, that the 'purer than pure' Blair regime could be bought for ready money.

The brothers Srichand and Gopichand Hinduja, sons of a self-made Indian billionaire, had come to live in London after making still more money, partly in the arms trade. Their applications for British citizenship had earlier been declined, with civil servants casting doubt on their 'good character' and questioning the origins of their fortune, but Gopichand received his passport soon after Blair became Prime Minister. After that their relationship with New Labour blossomed. They offered to sponsor the Faith Zone, which was perhaps the single most dismal part of the wretched Millennium Dome exhibition, whereupon Srichand got his passport too.

In November 1999 they entertained the Blairs, Mandelson, Jeffrey Archer and many other great names at a party for Diwali, the Hindu festival of light, where the guests were asked to sign the 'Hinduja pledge' to work for tolerance and peace, Blair presumably signing with his fingers crossed behind his back. Then rumours began to circulate that Mandelson had interceded on his friends' behalf at the Home Office, and Fleet Street sniffed a story. At first Alastair Campbell said that 'Mandelson had not got involved in the matter – beyond being asked to be involved, which he had refused to do', before someone at the Home Office told Campbell that Mandelson had in fact tried to push along Srichand's application. Mandelson denies to this day that this was so and says that the story was based on a confusion, and he might even be telling the truth.

What happened now was worthy not so much of Berlusconi's Sardinia as of Stalin's Kremlin. Like one Politburo member eyeing and circling another to ensure that the other comrade was shot instead of himself, Campbell let the lobby know that there were 'difficulties and contradictions' in Mandelson's account. In case Blair's nerve would fail when it came to sacking his old friend, Campbell then told the press that the Northern Ireland Secretary had gone before Mandelson himself knew.

There may have been a certain poetic justice in this. Dirty work at the crossroads was not unknown in Mandelson's own career. Right at the beginning of the Blair government the press discovered that Robin Cook, the new Foreign Secretary, was having a clandestine affair. Campbell broke up Cook's marriage by ordering him to choose immediately between his wife and his mistress, and Mandelson tried to distract media attention by leaking a completely false story that Chris Patten, the last governor of Hong Kong, might be prosecuted under the Official Secrets Act for writing about his years there.

Pretty straight guys. Even so, the departure of Mandelson was very telling. If Blair could allow his closest ally to be destroyed at Campbell's whim simply to gratify a passion for news management, what else might he be capable of?

Although the junta had pencilled in the first week of May as an election date since May four years earlier, the election was postponed until June because of the foot-and-mouth outbreak. Blair was obviously going to win, but something had gone wrong, and the conjuror was losing his magic touch. The previous year he had seemed to be still in tune with those populist values of the mass media when he came out grinning into Downing Street to announce the birth of his son Leo, holding in his hand a mug bearing the picture of one of his other children in violation of the code, on which politicians claim to be so keen, that images of children should never be published. But he had suffered a disconcerting humiliation when speaking to the Women's Institute, an admirable body far from merely devoted, as the received idea had it, to jam-making and home-making. When he patronisingly read out a vainglorious list of his government's achievements, the WI ladies grew restive and then began to slow-handclap him. He panicked, realising that he had lost his audience completely and that there were still some people in the country less servile and pliable than the Labour conference. That autumn came the petrol protests by farmers and lorry-drivers when, once again, Blair found that there were events he couldn't control by spin and evasion.

Never was the emptiness and nastiness of New Labour been so displayed as at the 2001 election. One of the first commentators to perceive Blair's potential well before he became party leader was Robert Harris, later rescued from the ordeal of newspaper life by becoming a best-selling novelist. He had been picked to accompany Blair on his triumphal campaign in 1997, and had written with deep admiration about the new Prime Minister. But four years is a long time in politics. As the next election approached Harris began a column with the memorable words 'There is something truly loathsome about the modern Labour Party'.

Several things prompted that spasm of disgust. The date of the election had been leaked to the *Sun* as a Campbell titbit before the Queen, the head of state, had been asked for a dissolution, a fine example of the populist values of the mass media. Then the junta arranged for Blair to speak at St Olave's, a girls' school in south London, with hymns sung and the Prime Minister standing in front of stained glass, which actually gave the impression of a halo. Just as the ladies of the WI had not known that Blair would be inflicting his dismal party propaganda on them, the headmistress hadn't been warned that his appearance would be the first shot in the election campaign, or that Blair, along with emetic pleas that 'I want not just to win your vote, but to win your heart and mind' would be exploiting those schoolgirls while he spouted tendentious soundbites: 'foundations laid for a brighter future . . . real progress .. beacons lit showing us a better way' and denigrated the opposition.

In June Labour won another huge victory, 413 seats to the Tories' pitiful 166. And yet even if the Tories remained unelectable, there was far more telling evidence that Blair's magic had gone: the all-important fact about the 2001 British general election was the precipitous collapse in voting turnout. Most observers had predicted that it would drop, but absolutely no one foresaw that it would plummet, from 72 per cent to 59 per cent.

Some decline in voting has been seen in many advanced countries. It's now a high turnout in presidential elections if half of Americans vote, although at the epic election of 1896, when William Jennings Bryan declaimed, 'You shall not crucify mankind upon a cross of gold,' almost 80 per cent of Americans (or the white males to whom the franchise was effectively confined) cast votes. In this country, figures in the upper 80 or even lower 90 per cents were recorded in individual constituencies early in the last century, and the highest national turnout at a general election was 84 per cent in 1950. Even in 2006, a general election in the Netherlands could see a turnout of just over 80 per cent.

A sophisticated argument can be made that low turnout is a 'problem of success', that fewer and fewer of us vote because we are ever more contented with our lot. The flaw in that has been pointed out by Susan Watkins of *New Left Review*: turnout is lowest, and still most sharply declining, in just those parts of the country which are the most depressed, in more senses of that word than one. Most of the British people today have never had it so good; but there remain large parts of our country which are, as Macaulay said of eighteenth-century Ireland, 'tranquil with the ghastly tranquillity of exhaustion and despair'.

In 2001 the problem went deeper. Labour's vote fell in the space of no more than four years from 13.5 to 10.7 million. At Blair's first victory, barely a third of the total electorate had voted for his party; now less than a quarter had. Was this the triumph of the 'Blair revolution', the 'project' and the Third Way? And was it a mandate for any more wars, let alone contentious and hazardous wars?

For all the inanity and vapidity of the books and essays written about Blair by his sycophants, the 'project' had had some electoral meaning. Blair wanted to repair the rift between Labour and Liberal traditions, but he also wanted to take the class out of politics. Until the late nineteenth century, Tories and Whigs had been patrician parties which relied on a middle-class electorate to chose which branch of the ruling class would govern them. But by the end of the century a political 'cleavage of classes' had developed, to the dismay of Lord Rosebery, who led a Liberal government as the last Whig. His colleague Sir William Harcourt had told him in 1894 that it was too late and that 'the horizontal division of parties was certain to come as a consequence of household suffrage', words which seemed more prescient in the next century when what became the two largest parties, Conservatives and Labour, were plainly distinguished by class.

This horizontal division had begun to erode under Margaret Thatcher when so many 'C2s', the increasingly prosperous upper working class personified by the (economically if not culturally) upwardly mobile 'Essex Man', and even many trade unionists had voted for her. In 1997 Blair had very successfully formed a new coalition of his own: loyal working-class voters, especially in the north of England and in Scotland, who had never deserted Labour; some of Thatcher's C2s; but also a large infusion of 'ABs', the professional and commercial middle classes whom Blair had done so much to woo.

They were sick of the Tories and knew that a vote for the Lib Dems was for a party which would never win an election. Blair offered them a wonderful alternative: 'Labour lite', a free-market economy, and no danger of higher income tax, all nicely packaged with a caring rhetoric about values and opportunity, an appeal to which much of the middle class had always been more susceptible than the more brutish Tories had ever realised.

Few people had ever loved Thatcher, but many thought that she was doing the country good, and she could always be defended on the Viennese saying that if you want the meat you have to pay for the bones: if you hoped to enjoy the fruits of her drastic economic liberation you had to put up with her rebarbative personality. Blair's genius had been to keep the Thatcherite meat and leave the Tories the bones; but now that meat itself was beginning to smell nasty.

It smelled bad when the apparat busily wheeled and dealed to get its favourites into Parliament. Mark Fisher, the Labour MP for Stoke-on-Trent Central, was approached by 'a senior party official' who offered him a peerage if he would stand down and make his seat available. Fisher was a strong supporter of an elected House of Lords and 'was outraged'. But in another case a carpetbagger was successfully jobbed in. Shaun Woodward was one of the choicest examples of those who gravitated towards the Blair junta.

Having worked as the Tories' director of communications during the 1992 election campaign, he married well – very well indeed – to a Sainsbury heiress. In this age of fluid party allegiances, his wife's uncle, Lord Sainsbury, first bankrolled the SDP in its David Owen days, much as if he were an eighteenth-century grandee like Rockingham paying for his private cabal in Parliament, but then became one of New Labour's largest donors, and then by happy coincidence minister responsible for science in the Blair government. On the Hollywood principle 'the son-in-law also rises', Woodward first entered Parliament as a Tory, before adroitly jumping ship to New Labour. A seat was found for him, and he was also told he could expect a government job, which he finally received in what Peter Oborne called 'a very rare example, much to be cherished, of Tony Blair keeping a promise'. But Woodward did have his moment of glory with his definition 'New Labour is a party for everyone, not of any particular class or any particular view'.

There has indeed been something very redolent of the Augustan age about life under Blair: not the literary genius or architectural grandeur – very much not those – but the jobbery and 'connexion'. Lord Drayson, one more large party donor who has done well out of government contracts, became defence minister, and it was all too characteristic of the age that John Birt and then Greg Dyke became director-general of the BBC, one obvious mountebank succeeding another. The BBC was meant to be at the proverbial arm's length from the government, but now it too was brought into the big tent: Birt actually went to work at Downing Street when he left the BBC, and Dyke was appointed director general after he made a large donation to New Labour. This was a big tent for people of no particular view, but with particular sums of money.

We must come back to Iraq

One of the hackneyed phrases beloved of political journalism is 'Events, dear boy, events,' even if Harold Macmillan never actually said it, any more than James

Callaghan actually said, 'Crisis, what crisis?' But events do happen, sometimes horrifically and unimaginably. Four months after Blair's first election victory Princess Diana was killed, three months after his second came the news from New York on 11 September 2001. Most of us can remember hearing it, and then – which is what made it the great defining moment of the new century – watching in real time as the vast towers collapsed, taking nearly 3,000 human lives as they fell.

Among sombre consequences of that act of mass murder was the response of the lumpenintelligentsia, the chattering liberal left. The Writers-with-a-capital-W were bad enough: 'Touch me,' besought Jeanette Winterson. 'Kiss me. Remind me what I am. Remind me that this life is the one we make together. The immensity of this event can only be mirrored in the immensity of what we are,' and although Martin Amis didn't ask to be kissed he did portray the lethal aircraft 'sharking in' amid 'world hum' to produce 'the worldflash of a coming future', before concluding a little disappointingly that he felt 'species shame'. Worse were those who blamed the victims: Mary Beard, a Cambridge classics don, could not repress 'the feeling that, however tactfully you dress it up, the United States had it coming' (not *very* tactfully, dear lady, as far as the bereaved of New York were concerned), and Rosie Boycott, who has edited not one but two national newspapers, thought that 'the West should take the blame for pushing people in third world countries to the end of their tether'.

In his own response, Blair very rightly not only expressed his solidarity with the American people but rebuked such nonsense. His support for the American action in Afghanistan followed naturally, and that action was – in the sharpest contrast to what was to come – legally justifiable, militarily feasible, and in any case politically inevitable. If the attack of 11 September had been the work of a recognisable state, like the attack of 7 December 1941, then no one could have denied that a state of war existed, as it had with Japan after Pearl Harbor. In the curious world we now inhabit, where state-sponsored terrorism has given way to terrorism-sponsored states, a campaign in Afghanistan was the next best thing, and in any case, as the chatterers never recognised, no American President who had failed to take military action after the carnage in New York could have remained in office.

But a grave mistake was made in Washington, and by Blair following the American lead. It was absurd to think of curing Afghanistan of all its ills, or building a Scandinavian democracy in the Pamirs. The right course of action was a short, sharp punitive campaign of the greatest speed and ferocity designed to collar Osama bin Laden, destroy Al-Qaeda, inflict as much pain and damage on the Taliban as possible, and then get out. What's more, it is almost certain that bin Laden could have been found, but for the first display of that ideologically driven incompetence of which there was to be so much more before long: Donald Rumsfeld was so absorbed with his intended move toward Iraq that he screwed up the central purpose of the mission in Afghanistan.

We didn't know that then. And nor did we know so much else that Blair knew. Having gone to Washington nine days after the Twin Towers fell, he was told by Bush about the coming war, according to Sir Christopher Meyer, who was present: 'When we've dealt with Afghanistan, we must come back to Iraq.'

Shortly after that Blair gave his weird speech – 'The kaleidoscope has been shaken' – at the Labour conference. But it was the rest of the peroration which had more simple-minded listeners in ecstasies. 'The starving, the wretched, the dispossessed, the ignorant, those living in want and squalor from the deserts of northern Africa to the slums of Gaza, to the mountain ranges of Afghanistan: they too are our cause.' Those words were cheered to the echo, and they were deeply dishonest. By talking about those living in want and squalor in Gaza, Blair was providing rhetorical cover for an American administration which cared very little for them but had other fish to fry.

For the moment, Blair could bask in adulation, at the Labour conference or in Washington. He was now more than 'the Prime Minister of the United States', he was an all-American hero. On that first visit to Washington after 11 September, Blair sat in the gallery while Bush addressed Congress. The President mentioned the Prime Minister, looked up and said, 'Thank you for coming, friend.' And the admiration united conservative Republicans with liberals who were perplexed about the woes of the world and were captivated by what they thought of as Blair's eloquence, such a contrast to their own tongue-tied President. Before long a book could be published, by a London journalist writing for American readers, called *Tony Blair: The Making of a World Leader*. All this hero-worship was finally turning Blair's head.

Displaying further detachment from reality, eagerness to ingratiate himself in America, and sheer ignorance of history, he told a stricken New York: 'My father's generation knew what it was like. They went through the Blitz,' and went on, 'there was one country and one people that stood side by side with us then. That country was America, and the people were the American people.'

'The Blitz' was the name popularly given to the bombing of London and other British cities in the autumn and winter of 1941–2. At that time, many countries 'stood side by side with us': the dominions – Canada, Australia, New Zealand, South Africa – whose parliaments had voted to join the war in September 1939; hundreds of thousands of Indian volunteers; the exiled governments of Europe – Czechoslovakia, Poland, the Netherlands, Denmark, Norway and Free France – with their fighting forces; and Greece, which was as yet undefeated in an heroic struggle with the Axis. Come to think of it, apart from Soviet Russia, just about the only important country on earth which was not 'side by side with us' that winter was the United States, which was very profitably neutral.

Whenever he can, Blair invokes Hitler and his crimes. He supported a new Holocaust Day, 'a day when the country reflects on the terrible and evil deeds in the world', as he put it with solemn triteness. And in his usual vein of do-it-yourself history he said that 'you go back to the Thirties, to the start of the persecution of the Jewish people, the murders and the wholesale plunder of their wealth and you think these things were there in 1935, 1934 even, and it was only in 1939 that they got round to doing something. They said this has got to be stopped. I think there are some interesting reflections on all that.' An even more interesting reflection was that Blair had no idea what he was talking about: no one said in 1939 that we are going to war because Hitler's persecution has got to be stopped. This is a man who makes up history as well as policy as he goes along.

Inspired by such lofty sentiments and rewritten history, Blair now said that 'however tough' it might be, he would fight alongside the United States with 'no grandstanding, no offering implausible and impractical advice from the touchline . . . We will stay with you to the last.' As events would prove, the White House and Pentagon could have used a little advice from a candid friend. But in any case, when Blair said that, he was writing a blank cheque. With those words he quite simply renounced national sovereignty. For all the flattering talk about leadership of the free world, he was no longer a leader of anything or anyone; by his own choice, he was ready to be led anywhere.

Lies, damned lies and dossiers

If I'm being honest

Having defined the Blair regime when he said that 'New Labour is intensely relaxed about people getting filthy rich', Peter Mandelson bequeathed another deathless saying. At the 2001 election he made a poignant speech about fighting, not quitting, and then did quit: in the autumn of 2004 he received two successive appointments, to the Stewardship of the Manor of Northstead (the legal fiction by which an MP resigns his seat) and then, rather more importantly, a European Commissionership, which was in Blair's gift, and in which office he would show his considerable ability. When he accepted the Brussels job, Mandelson said as an aside, 'If I'm being honest, which I will be – I don't think I've got anything to lose by being honest at this stage in my political career.' It was an almost endearing, and certainly a very revealing, turn of phrase, as though 'being honest' was an avocation like golf or gardening which a chap might take up in middle age when he had nothing better to do.

But his old friend and master had most certainly not taken up being honest at this stage in his political career, and he had everything to lose by telling the truth. As soon as he had committed the country to war, Blair embarked on a calculated campaign of deception and falsehood. This was not an accident or a whim, it was implicit in his position. The Tories were later advised that their line on the war should be 'right to fight, wrong to lie', but this, though it sounded neat, entirely missed the point and made an illusory distinction. The Iraq war was not only fought on a confection of falsehood, it had to be; and it was the Blair junta's war of lies preceding the war itself which ensured that that the enterprise was morally bankrupt from the start.

To understand what happened, first ask why the Iraq war took place. The answer is not hard as historical questions go. A group of politically formidable, ideologically zealous Americans whom we know as the neoconservatives had wanted a war of revenge to destroy Saddam for at least twelve years past. They had been advocating it publicly for eight years, as anyone could see by reading their journals such as the *Weekly Standard*, and this is very much to their credit. Those Americans have been widely abused, and 'neocon' has become not so much a fighting word as a curse, sometimes with ethnic overtones.

And yet, just as Blair comes out of Iraq not better than Bush but far worse, the American neocons come out of Iraq far and away better than those British politicians and commentators, including the majority of Labour MPs, who supported the war. Given the state of Iraq today, one can scarcely say that the neocons knew what they were doing, but they knew what they wanted: the destruction of Saddam as such, whether he were armed with an array of nuclear warheads or no more than pop-guns and peashooters. The purpose of their war would be regime change for the sake of regime change. They might have been right. But how many Labour MPs wanted that? And why had not Blair been likewise openly advocating military intervention to destroy Saddam?

A working alliance was formed between such men as Paul Wolfowitz, Richard Perle and Douglas Feith and another group led by Donald Rumsfeld and Dick Cheney, not doctrinaire neocons but nationalistic militarists who wanted to restore American might and prestige after all the demoralising years that followed Vietnam and Watergate and who for some reason weren't content with a resounding Western victory in the Cold War. These men attached themselves to George Bush the Younger and came to power after his first presidential election victory, such as it was. Indeed if one were to ask the question 'Who took the decision to invade Iraq?' a good answer would be 'The Supreme Court'. The court's capricious decision to award the disputed election to Bush rather than Al Gore (who won more popular votes nationally, and might well have carried Florida, and the electoral college, if the election there had been scrupulously conducted) meant that there would be an invasion.

We know from the evidence of two members of Bush's original cabinet, Richard Clarke and Paul O'Neill, that a campaign to destroy Saddam was being discussed as soon as Bush was inaugurated. According to O'Neill, Rumsfeld, the new Defence Secretary, told a National Security Council meeting in February 2001 that regime change in Iraq was the first step towards transforming the Middle East. All that was needed was the opportunity, and that came on 11 September. If the murderous attacks were a plausible reason for an operation in Afghanistan, they had nothing whatever to do with Iraq and provided no possible justification for an invasion of that country. And yet, although 11 September was in no sense a *casus belli* where Iraq was concerned, for the Bush administration it was a pretext, or perhaps what journalists call a peg, an occasion for something long planned.

Everyone could see that there had been a turn in American policy when Bush reached the White House. One admirer defined it as an aggressive foreign policy based on unapologetic nationalism, another as 'the projection of American power in America's interests'. There had been no such open turn in British policy, and no single Labour candidate at the 2001 election had proposed a war on Iraq. But then Blair's policy by now amounted to the protection of British power in America's interests.

Every defence of him over Iraq disintegrates not merely because of what we have learned about his regime's deceit and mendacity but by applying the elementary historical principle of chronology. In his own mind he manages to confuse and jumble the sequence of events, but that's all the more reason why no one else should do so. It sometimes seems to be forgotten that Blair became Prime Minister in May 1997, when Bush still had nearly four years to go in the governor's mansion in Austin.

We were often to be told, not least by Blair, that 'everything changed on 11 September', a fatuous and dishonest phrase. In fact nothing whatever changed on 11 September, not in the sense intended, not in terms of the political situation in Iraq or in the larger region or of the objective reasons for an invasion. There were no better arguments of any kind for military action against Saddam on 12 September 2001 than there had been on 10 September. Where everything *did* change, of course, was in terms of American politics. With the nation in a state of shock, the Bush administration was able to cow its critics, overawe Congress and terrify the public.

In September 2001 Blair was told by Bush that they would 'come back to Iraq' after Afghanistan, which they duly did. And here began the great crime of Blair's career: he knew that an invasion of Iraq was the President's plan, but he did not communicate this to the British people, or to Parliament, or even to his Cabinet colleagues. In public he sent Americans into raptures with his language of standing shoulder to shoulder, and he then managed to persuade most of his own followers, at least for a while. But then Blair had grasped the truth that 'you can fool some of the people all of the time, you can fool all of the people some of the time – and those are good odds'.

What happened over the eighteen months from September 2001 to March 2003 is by now history, which does not make the story any less outrageous. American plans for war proceeded apace, and stepped up a gear in the spring. Bush summoned Blair to his retreat in west Texas, and thither Blair went. A detailed operation wasn't planned at that time – although American preparations for an invasion were already openly underway – but what happened at Crawford is quite clear. We have no documentary evidence about the meeting at Crawford as yet but it will transpire soon: whatever else is said about the United States, it is a free country, and official archives become available much more quickly in Washington than in London. In any case the outcome of the meeting is apparent. There were no oaths of blood-brotherhood between Bush and Blair, the President did not need to recall the arcane initiation rituals of the Skull and Bones society at Yale, there were no Protocols of the Elders of Crawford. Instead, the President told the Prime Minister that an invasion of Iraq was now certain, and in reply Blair said that Bush could rely on his total support, military as well as moral. The only trouble was that Blair told nobody else.

As it happened, at just that time there was a fascinating vignette which illustrated the Blair junta's methods, after the death of the Queen Mother. Her death and funeral discomposed some progressive commentators, who had sneeringly predicted that it would pass almost unnoticed, but in the event there was a great outpouring of national emotion, as sincere as the incontinent grief for Diana had been synthetic.

This was as much a collective memory of a prouder age, the finest hour of 1940, as a tribute to an old lady, and needless to say the junta wanted to cash in on it. Downing Street suggested that a prominent role at the obsequies should again be assigned to the Prime Minister but this time there was a brush-off. When this was mentioned almost in passing by the journalist Peter Oborne, Alastair Campbell exploded, in a foretaste of the Gilligan–Kelly affair a year later, and demanded a complete retraction.

The official in charge of protocol was a retired Army officer known as Black Rod. He was told by the junta to corroborate their mendacious version of events but, coming of a generation with different standards, he declined. In the end, Downing Street backed down, and a statement was put out which Campbell said – again falsely – vindicated him, when in fact it showed that he had been lying. Trivial in itself, this episode gave a frightening intimation of what might be expected when Downing Street told brazen falsehoods on a far graver subject.

A war of lies was already being waged by the Bush administration to persuade the American people that Saddam had an advanced programme for building 'weapons of mass destruction', and that he was connected to Islamic terrorism in general and 11 September in particular. This last was done by indirect persuasion or subliminal advertising, with Bush mentioning 'Iraq' and '9/11' as many times as possible in close proximity, sometimes more than ten times each in the same speech. The result was that by the spring of 2003 a majority of Americans said they believed that Saddam was connected with the New York attack, although this was something which no member of the Bush administration ever said in plain terms, since they knew it wasn't true.

Apart from softening up the public, Bush browbeat Congress with threats, cajolery, even plain bullying, and the open insinuation that anyone who opposed the his plans was un-American or downright disloyal. So it was that in October 2002 Congress cravenly passed an 'Authorisation for the Use of Military Force against Iraq', allowing the President to take action 'as he determines to be necessary and appropriate', not to say to do anything he damn well liked. In April 1917 and again in December 1941, the President said that a state of war existed, but war was not formally declared until Congress had debated and voted on it. Writing as an American, Michael Kinsley has said that this renunciation by Congress of its right to declare war is the gravest constitutional crisis in generations, and Americans are now coming to terms with the way they were misled by their rulers, the 'shock and awe' with which Bush, Cheney, Rumsfeld steamrollered their way to war.

Meantime, a comparable and in some ways more insidious and iniquitous war of lies was being waged on this side of the Atlantic. Having privately committed the country to war, Blair had to sell the coming invasion to Parliament and people, which he and his clique at Downing Street set about doing in shameless fashion, exaggerating and distorting whatever evidence could be found to justify the claims that Saddam possessed 'weapons of mass destruction' and that he represented, in Blair's fatal words – perhaps the most untruthful ever uttered by a British Prime Minister – a 'serious and current' threat to this country.

The two high – or low – points were the 'dossiers' presented in September 2002 and February 2003. Both were concocted by Downing Street using information extracted from the intelligence services under duress, though using other material besides. The authors of these dossiers were John Scarlett, chairman of the Joint Intelligence Committee, and his friend Alastair Campbell, a man whom a High Court judge had once described as an unreliable witness.

The first dossier claimed that 'as a result of the intelligence we judge that Iraq has sought significant quantities of uranium from Africa, despite having no active civil nuclear power programme that could require it' and that Iraq had chemical and biological arms which were not only weaponised, in the phrase, but ready for instant deployment: 'The document discloses that his military planning allows for some WMD to be ready within forty-five minutes of an order to use them.' This was simply Campbell the cheap tabloid hack looking for a headline, and he found it: '45 minutes from attack', the *Evening Standard* trumpeted.

No one stopped to examine the very phrase 'weapons of

mass destruction'. It's a quite recent coining, and a fraudulent one designed to obfuscate rather than illuminate. 'WMD' is held to embrace everything from nuclear warheads, which can obliterate a city in the twinkling of an eye, to mustard gas, which the British Army used in the Great War on the specific ground that it was more humane than machine-guns or shells. Fortunately for all of us, producing nuclear devices requires not only scientific expertise but large industrial resources, whereas a nerve gas such as sarin can be manufactured on a kitchen table by anyone with a modest knowledge of chemistry.

And any idea that 'WMD' are uniquely dangerous is easily disproved. In 1945, fewer than 200,000 people were killed, albeit in the most dramatic and frightful way, at Hiroshima and Nagasaki, but this was at the end of a war in which well over a million Germans and Japanese had already been incinerated or asphyxiated by 'conventional' bombing. It would have been little consolation to those dying in the firestorms of Hamburg and Tokyo to know that there was nothing 'mass-destructive' about their deaths.

More recently, in the 1990s, there was something like a controlled experiment, or compare-and-contrast, in east Asia: two terrorist attacks, both on metros or underground railways, one in South Korea and one in Tokyo. In the Japanese case, a gang of crazy religious cultists attacked the metro with 'WMD' in the form of sarin; in Korea the terrorists used conventional or non-mass-destructive weaponry in the form of a Molotov cocktail, a plastic milk carton filled with petrol. The 'WMD' attack killed twelve people, the non-'WMD' attack killed 120. Finally there was the logically bizarre invocation of 'weapons of mass destruction' to whip up panic after the 11 September massacre. The victims in New York were killed by a handful of bloodthirsty religious maniacs armed with tiny knives. When did box-cutters become 'WMD'?

Then in February came the second document, soon immortalised as the 'dodgy dossier'. It turned out to be a combination of intelligence, sections from a *Jane's Intelligence Review* report on Iraq, and parts of a graduate thesis based on twelve-year-old public information, which Campbell and his colleagues downloaded from the internet, typographical errors and all, and altogether a fine piece of work by that unsatisfactory witness.

At this time Robin Cook was still in the Cabinet, but weeks later, when he had resigned, he recalled thinking that the first dossier was very feeble stuff: 'I was taken aback at how thin the dossier was. There was a striking absence of any recent and alarming firm intelligence. The great majority was derivative.' He added, 'The plain fact is that a lot of the intelligence in the dossier turned out to be wrong.' In June, Campbell was obliged to write an apologetic letter to the intelligence chiefs, acknowledging that information had been mishandled and vowing that in the future 'far greater care would be taken in dealing with anything that might impact on their reputation or their work'. But by this time the dossiers had done their work and British troops were in Iraq.

More chilling details

Although Blair had said that a second United Nations resolution would be necessary before hostilities began, he managed to evade that undertaking when it was clear that there wouldn't be one, and so did most Labour MPs who had made so much of the UN. The Commons twice debated the invasion and voted on it. On 26 February, the ministerial motion supported 'the government's continuing efforts in the United Nations to disarm Iraq of its weapons of mass destruction' and demanded that Iraq should 'recognise this as its final opportunity to comply with the its disarmament obligations'; there was a hostile amendment saying that the case for military action was 'as yet unproven'. Labour MPs voted 274 for the motion, 60 against, the Tories 152 for, none against; on the amendment, Labour was 255 to 122 against, the Tories 130 to 14.

Then on 18 March, just as the invasion was about to begin, there was another debate and two more divisions. A lengthy ministerial motion said that the government should now 'use all means necessary to ensure the disarmament of Iraq's weapons of mass destruction' and offered 'wholehearted support to the men and women of the armed forces' who were 'now on duty in the Middle East'. This passed by 256 Labour votes to 85, and 147 Tories to 3. An amendment saying that 'the case for war against Iraq has not yet been established' was defeated by 247 to 139 Labour votes, with 140 to 16 Tories. On all these divisions the Liberal Democrats voted solidly against the war and the government would have been defeated if the Tories, apart from a distinguished minority, had not rolled over. As it was, the 139 Labour dissidents composed the largest rebellion in a governing party since the Liberals split over Home Rule in 1886.

We shall never know how many MPs truly believed Blair's case, or how many Cabinet ministers did, although it is a fair surmise that only a minority of Labour MPs really wanted the war. Cook resigned, and others might have done if they had had the courage, but they decided instead, as Lloyd George would have said, to perish with their drawn salaries in their hands. Some wobbled a the last moment, with Jack Straw, Cook's more pliant successor as Foreign Secretary, wondering whether it was really necessary for British troops to be committed. It is whispered that Gordon Brown was sceptical and tempered his criticisms only because he wanted to keep his job as Chancellor. We shall doubtless hear from other ministers about the private reservations they harboured when they come to publish their self-serving memoirs.

Not that politicians were alone. The press broadly supported the war, the Murdoch papers in violent terms. As early as 10 September 2002 – a couple of weeks before the government's infamous dossier – the *Sun* wrote that 'recognition of the necessity of an Allied strike on Iraq is growing as more chilling details of Saddam Hussein's weapons of mass destruction are revealed'. Another leader, on 15 March 2003, baldly stated that 'Saddam has stockpiled weapons of mass destruction, and he's not going to give them up', and the paper's columnists were equally sure of themselves. On 14 January 2003 Richard Littlejohn wrote, 'Don't kid yourself. There's going to be war in Iraq unless Saddam Hussein hands over his weapons of mass destruction. He's got them. We know he's got them. He knows we know he's got them.' And so elsewhere in the press, David Aaronovitch wrote in the *Guardian* that if there proved to be no 'WMD' he would never believe anything the government ever said again, while Max Hastings told readers of the *Daily Mail* that 'Tony Blair has taken a brave decision, that the only hope of influencing American behaviour is to share in American actions'.

Many of those who then rushed in later repented and angrily denounced Blair, but it is hard to feel much sympathy for those who say they were deceived. Anyone who actually believed what Blair said was not intellectually equipped to be a member of a parish council, let alone a great or once great parliamentary assembly, or for that matter to write for a parish newspaper. The blatancy of the imposture was so utterly obvious.

We sceptics were not blessed with any special intelligence, in either sense of the word, but we liked to think that we weren't born yesterday, and we could see what was happening in front of our eyes. We also had the advantage, it seemed, of a modest capacity for observation and for learning from experience. Having followed him carefully for some years, we had become aware that any statement at all was the less plausible or credible if it was made by Anthony Blair than otherwise. He was capable of saying absolutely anything, and 'he always means it at the time'. He had meant it when he had said that he had been a stowaway as a young boy even though he had not been, he had meant it when he said he had voted to ban hunting even though he had not done so, and now he meant it when he said that Saddam had 'WMD'.

One other absurd phrase would be bandied about when no 'WMD' came to light: there had been 'intelligence failures' before the war. But there were no failures; it was a complete success. The intelligence services did as they were told, just as the Attorney General did when he changed a first opinion that an invasion would be illegal. It was ridiculous for anyone not to see this, let alone for Mary Ann Sieghart later to write a column later in the *Times* headed 'Sack the spooks' about 'the failure of MI6 to get its facts right about Saddam's weapons of mass destruction', or for Timothy Garton Ash to write another in the *Guardian* headed 'Scarlett must go', saying that Scarlett was directly responsible for the false prospectus on which Britain went to war in Iraq,' as though Scarlett had malevolently misled an innocent and unwilling Blair.

If Blair was allowed to get away with this imposture it was partly because the wrong question was being asked. To ask what weaponry Saddam possessed was to hand Blair the advantage, and to allow him an excuse. But the question was not: What weaponry does Saddam possess? It should have been: Is Saddam's weaponry the real reason for a war on which we are plainly about to embark or is it a pretext concocted after a decision for war had already been taken? And so the crucial question in turn was and remains: *When was the decision for war taken?*

What had actually happened was reminiscent of two moments in classic movies. Everyone quotes Captain Renault's 'Shocked, shocked' and 'Round up the usual suspects', both of which might be given a rest by now. But

Claude Rains has a more interesting line as the police chief in *Casablanca*, after the demise in custody of the unfortunate character played by Peter Lorre: 'We haven't quite decided yet whether he committed suicide or died trying to escape.' He was dead, but they hadn't quite decided how; Bush and Blair were going to invade Iraq, but they hadn't quite decided why: 'WMD', terrorism, democracy, whatever.

What Blair ludicrously called 'my decision' for war was of course taken for him in Washington, as Jimmy Carter among others pointed out. After that, it was a matter of helping to find what Paul Wolfowitz memorably called 'bureaucratic reasons', or cosmetic excuses, to justify the invasion. And there Blair was able to perform a very useful service for President Bush, at the expense of the integrity of his own intelligence services as well as any reputation he ever possessed for honesty.

This was prefigured in *Citizen Kane* (using an incident said to be taken from the real life of William Randolph Hearst), when Kane's newspaper is fomenting what became the Spanish–American War of 1898, and his correspondent is sent to Cuba for that purpose. 'Girls delightful. Could send you prose poems about scenery,' the man cables back to the paper's office, but 'there is no war'. To which Kane replies – in exactly the sense Blair conveyed to Scarlett – 'You provide the prose poems. I'll provide the war.' And so they both did.

When it later became clear that there was no such weaponry in Iraq, suspicions began to harden about what had happened. On the morning of 29 May 2003, there was an item on the Radio 4 *Today* programme shortly after the 6.00 news in which Andrew Gilligan, the defence correspondent, said that the intelligence services had been unhappy about the way the claims about WMD had been 'sexed up', citing one intelligence source who said that he and his colleagues were dissatisfied at how their information had been used or misused.

What now ensued was one of the most disgusting episodes in recent British history. Alastair Campbell was hysterically angry about the story, which had been presented in a slipshod way, but which was in essence true and far too near the knuckle. He determined to 'fuck Gilligan', as he characteristically put it, and was not discouraged by his good Christian Prime Minister. The Downing Street cabal now worked tirelessly to 'out' the source. He was David Kelly, smeared after his death by a Downing Street spokesman as 'a Walter Mitty figure' but in fact one of the most eminent authorities in the country on chemical and biological weaponry. He was duly outed, he appeared very unhappily before a Commons committee, and then, unable to bear the strain, he killed himself. It is hard to deny that Campbell and Blair had his blood on their hands, but since they soon had so much more, why would they care?

An inquiry was set up under the Northern Ireland judge Lord Hutton, who heard evidence from many people and took a long time to produce a report the following year which was splendidly at variance with the evidence he had heard and was quite rightly damned as a whitewash. Hutton effectively admitted that. It became clear during the course of the inquiry that Blair had in fact been privy to the decision to 'out' Kelly, and had thus brazenly lied when he said otherwise. He should have been recalled for further examination, but as the dutiful judge later said, there was then the possibility that 'various allegations would be put to the Prime Minister. There would be glaring headlines about the allegations and I did not think it would be appropriate to do that.' But Hutton could not help letting us learn what had gone on. Those who covered the whole hearing (which the populace were not considered grown up enough to see televised) said that many of the witnesses were unimpressive. Blair was ill at ease and Geoff Hoon, the fatuous Defence Secretary, was downright shifty, as well he might have been.

But John Scarlett was by contrast entirely relaxed when he gave evidence in August, as he accepted full 'authorship' for the dossiers presented before the invasion, in effect saying, 'All my own work.' Naturally enough, the Downing Street junta immediately claimed this as vindication, saying that the Prime Minister had been exonerated. Sir Malcolm Rifkind, the former Tory Cabinet minister, was regrettably out of Parliament at the time, having lost his Edinburgh seat in the Tories' Scottish wipe-out of 1997 and failed to win it back four years later, finally returning to the Commons for a London seat. But from outside the Commons he had condemned the invasion when it began as 'a most foolish and unnecessary war'.

On the evening of Scarlett's testimony Rifkind appeared on *Channel 4 News* and grasped the point with the authority of a former Defence Secretary and Foreign Secretary, as well as the acuity of the Scots advocate he had once been. So far from exculpating Downing Street, Scarlett's testimony was in itself profoundly incriminating, since it showed the degree to which under the Blair junta the intelligence services had been politicised or even corrupted. The spooks and spymasters used to take high professional pride in their work: gathering, collating and assessing raw intelligence which was then furnished to their political masters in the government, but always at arm's length and (in another favourite phrase, as Rifkind recalled) with 'a health warning', emphasising that even the best such intelligence must be incomplete, and should be treated with care.

What had happened in the case of Iraq was back to front, in the manner of *Alice in Wonderland*: 'sentence first, then verdict'. Or in this case, the decision for war had come first and then the reasons for it. As a logician might say, it illustrated the difference between induction and deduction. Blair had not begun (though this is what he pretended to have done) with an objective review of the practical evidence from which he inferred the necessity of an invasion. He had begun a priori with a premiss: he was going to support Washington in whatever decision Bush took, and would then search for any evidence which could be adduced to justify that decision.

This was the heart of the matter. Not only we been taken to war on a false prospectus, on specious pretexts, or in plainer English on a lie; the falsity of Blair's position was deeper still: it was not his claims as such about 'WMD' but his larger case that for almost a year he had not yet committed the country to war, when in fact he had, not to say his grotesque claim that he was 'doing everything I can to work for peace', when he was doing all he could to work for war.

Long since he had acquired a reputation, if not for being two faced, then for being a political chameleon, for wanting to be all things to all men, for misrepresenting the position to different sides, giving Unionists in Ulster to understand one thing and republicans another, using a different manner and even accent for different audiences, the Labour conference or the Commons, *Newsnight* on some grave subject or a chat show when he was being folksy. And even Blair's admirers conceded there was some truth in this, though Roy Jenkins did so in sympathetic terms, saying that 'the human heart has many chambers' and that Blair's chameleon gift was no bad thing.

Then came Iraq, and even some of Blair's detractors now said that this charge for once did not apply. Whatever you thought of the war, whether or not you approved Blair's position, this time he had stood up to be counted, and had not changed colours or said one thing here and another there. But to the contrary, Iraq was the supreme and most disastrous demonstration of that very propensity on Blair's part: at the crucial point of his career, and indeed of his whole life, *he told Parliament publicly something different from what he had told President Bush privately.*

Even now Blair defends his decision with the circular argument that the war 'was the right thing to do', and he insists that Iraq is a better place today, a harder line to take all the time. But in the process he comes close to using Stanley Baldwin's line (as wittily paraphrased by the cartoonist Low): 'If I hadn't told you I wouldn't bring you here, you wouldn't have come.' It was the right thing to do; he couldn't have done it if he had told the truth; so lying was the right thing to do as well.

Finest moment

Stuff happens

As the invasion of Iraq was about to begin, Blair was at his
most exalted: 'Let the day-to-day judgements come and
go. Be prepared to be judged by history.' This had become
one of his favourite turns of phrase in one variant or other.
He was addicted to saying that 'history will be my judge',
to which one answer might have been, 'No, Prime
Minister, in a democracy we will.' But in any case, history
was about to make a judgement on the Iraq enterprise,
much faster and much harsher than Blair could have
guessed or feared; never has anyone been so horribly
undone by vanity, or even megalomania.

Despite Blair's insistence on supporting Washington
militarily, there were precedents for not doing so, and we
now know that Blair did not need to send British soldiers.
Some close to him didn't want to do so, and Blair's
political troops were unsteady on parade. Robin Cook
made it clear that he would resign from the Cabinet and
then did so, as did Clare Short, though too late to do any
good and after a painful display of girly tantrums, when
she declared at one point, 'I've done my turmoil.'

Several other members of the Cabinet privately sympathised with Cook and might have stopped Blair in his
tracks, and stopped his war, if they had resigned also.
Cook had been demoted from the Foreign Secretaryship
after the 2001 election, when his absolute reliability was
already suspect. But even Jack Straw counselled caution:
might we not offer all support short of military forces? He

must have had in mind Harold Wilson, who said that he sympathised with the American war in Vietnam, to the rage of the Labour left, but adroitly avoided sending British troops. Troops were what President Lyndon Johnson wanted. He was trying to form a coalition of the willing (as it wasn't then called) of at least token forces from different nations, and Australians as well as Thais did fight in Vietnam. An English visitor to Washington was later angrily told by Dean Rusk, the Secretary of State, 'All we wanted was one goddam battalion of the Black Watch,' but he didn't get them, thanks to the canny and elusive Wilson.

Nearly forty years on, the British Prime Minister was given a chance to stand aside honourably. Donald Rumsfeld had not long before been informed by Geoff Hoon, his British opposite number, that Great Britain enjoyed something called parliamentary government and that the Prime Minister needed a majority in the House of Commons, which evidently came to the American as a revelation. On the point of war Rumsfeld said that British troops weren't needed anyway, which wasn't merely tactless but insulting and humiliating. In November 2006 Kendall Myers, a senior State Department analyst, remembered what Rumsfeld had said as a 'clarifying moment' in the embarrassing Anglo-American relationship: 'That was the giveaway. I felt a little ashamed and a certain sadness that we had treated him [Blair] like that. And yet, here it was, there was nothing – no payback, no sense of a reciprocity of the relationship.' Many people in England saw that; Americans like Myers see that; Blair has never seen it.

Even Bush himself dimly perceived Blair's political difficulties and said privately that he would let Blair drop out of the invading coalition if it would help: they would find some other occupation for the 41,000 British military personnel in the region. But nothing would stop the eager warrior: 'I said I'm with you. I mean it.' When Bush repeated the offer, Blair said that he appreciated it, but 'I absolutely believe in this, too', and then, in the words which gave him such a thrill, 'I'm there to the very end.' British troops set off to fight and die in some foreign field, in order to gratify Blair's fantasies and to fulfil his empty rhetoric. This time the Black Watch would be there.

At first, 'the very end' didn't look so bad. There were initial setbacks when some of those who opposed the war allowed the wish to father the thought and foolishly predicted military failure for the invading forces, until those forces prevailed easily enough, as they were always going to given the immense disparity in men, armaments and sheer money between the United States and Iraq. The GIs stormed into Baghdad, Saddam's statue was toppled – and Blair, more messianic than ever, said, 'When people look back on this time, I honestly believe they will see this as one of the finest moments of our century.'

He didn't go so far as to mimic Bush's grotesque 'Mission Accomplished' stunt on 1 May, when a President whose experience of combat flying had been protecting Texas from Oklahoma when he was in the National Guard as a way of avoiding service in Vietnam, landed on the deck of an aircraft carrier to rapturous cheers. Maybe the Royal Navy couldn't spare a ship for Blair, or maybe there is a residual English sense of the ridiculous.

country. In December 2006, Hoon claimed that London had in fact warned the Americans about these errors, which only illustrates Blair's impotent irrelevance. Either he blindly followed the Americans, believing in magic as Doris Lessing put it, or he warned Washington and was completely ignored.

As 2003 wore on, it became steadily clearer that no magic was working. An operation which was misconceived in the first place was being gravely misconducted, like Suez but on a much vaster scale.

The echoes of 1956 were indeed many. In the summer of 2004 I was talking on a radio programme about a long essay on Blair and Iraq that I had written for the *Atlantic Monthly*, and one of my distant interlocutors was Anthony Sampson, the writer and journalist, who sadly died not long afterwards. At the time of Suez I was a young boy but Sampson was already a working newspaperman, and so when I mentioned Iraq and Suez in the same breath I was interested to see what his reaction would be.

Absolutely right, he said: there was a close resemblance between the two, and what's more, 'in both cases we are entitled to talk of a conspiracy'. Western governments are enraged by a troublesome Arab dictator and decide to settle the score. But the political circumstances mean that they cannot openly avow what they are doing and so they embark on subterfuge and deception.

One reluctant defender of Blair said something unintentionally revealing because quite untrue: the government might have exaggerated the case for war, but that's what governments always do as wars begin. To the contrary, governments have habitually exaggerated the

109

case for peace. In 1854, the Crimean War began against every wish of the Prime Minister, Lord Aberdeen, who ever after thought that he had been morally stained by the war. He later asked to be excused from paying for the rebuilding of a church on his estate, citing King David's refusal to rebuild the Temple because he had 'shed blood abundantly'. Then in 1899 the Boer War began even though the Prime Minister, Lord Salisbury, thought that the war had been engineered on behalf of 'people whom we despise, and for territory which will bring no profit and no power to England'. But then Aberdeen and Salisbury were Christians of a different sort from Blair.

Twice in the past century we entered great and historically decisive wars, on both occasions with the greatest possible reluctance on behalf of the government of the day. The Asquith Cabinet didn't go to war in 1914 until the German violation of Belgium and the turn in parliamentary and public opinion left no option. In 1939, the Cabinet, and especially Chamberlain himself, didn't want to go to war until the German invasion of Poland and the turn in parliamentary and public opinion again left no option.

There is in fact just one other occasion of modern times when a government wilfully exaggerated the case for war, and that is Suez. In 1956, the British were incensed when Colonel Gamal Nasser seized the Suez Canal, the French hated him because he had incited the nationalist rebellion in Algeria, and the Israelis saw him as their mortal enemy. A Cabinet committee on Suez set up in the summer of that year recorded on 30 July that the imme-diate aim was 'to bring down the present Egyptian government' – or to effect regime change, as we now say – but rather than proclaim that, or even say that they were attacking Egypt in order to regain control of the canal, London and Paris entered into a conspiracy of baroque complexity, outlined at Chequers and finalised in the greatest secrecy at a villa at Sèvres, outside Paris, on 22 October. Israel would attack Egypt and then the British and French – seemingly without any foreknowledge of that attack – would arrive to interpose themselves between the warring parties, and, as it conveniently happened, to take back the canal. And so, to borrow a later phrase, the facts were fixed to suit the case. Although the timescale is different in the case of Iraq, the pattern is the same. Instead of Sèvres there was Crawford, where, on 6 April 2002 as on 22 October 1956, the die had been cast.

Before long, Suez became a byword for political stupidity as well as deception. 'We had not realised', wrote David Astor, the owner-editor of the *Observer*, in a famous leader published even before the landings, and in words which that paper should have repeated as the invasion of Iraq was beginning, 'that our government was capable of such folly and crookedness'. Truly Suez ended in fiasco and humiliation, it was 'no end of a lesson', the line from Kipling which the Tory politician Anthony Nutting called his book about Suez, after he had resigned from the government in protest at 'a sordid manoeuvre, which was morally indefensible and politically suicidal', words just as apt today.

Even apter words had been written that November by Evelyn Waugh in a letter to his friend Anne Fleming (wife of the author Ian). He had brooded about Suez and reduced it to 'the important facts (a) it cannot be justified on moral or legal grounds (b) practically no recent action of any British government can be justified morally . . . (c) Any troup of Boy Scouts can defeat the Egyptian army (d) No one can govern Egypt now that Nasser has armed the schoolchildren', meaning that Nasser had encouraged Egyptian youth to take up arms.

That novelist's insight would have been useful at the Pentagon – or in Downing Street – in 2003. Once again, the problem wasn't the immediate military operation against the Iraqi army: a troup of Boy Scouts could pretty well have beaten them. It was the sequel, when 'the schoolchildren' – or armed zealots – made the country ungovernable. Suez might have been no end of a lesson, but not a single lesson had been learned. Blair certainly hadn't grasped what General Sir Charles Keightley, the commander in chief of the allied forces in 1956, said afterwards. However successful in 'pure military' terms, the venture will fail without the support of international opinion, and 'the one overriding lesson of the Suez operations is that world opinion is now an absolute principle of war and must be treated as such'.

With all those similarities, there are differences, and Anthony Eden comes far better out of Suez than Anthony Blair out of Iraq. The Suez adventure was a debacle but a short-lived one, from which the country soon recovered, whereas the cost of Iraq is incalculable but immense and will do vast damage to this country as well as the United States for many years to come.

Then again, the deception behind the Suez expedition, though grievous, was much less prolonged and in the end less damaging that the deception on which the Iraq war was launched. Even if Eden's *ruse de guerre* was foolish, most Tory MPs and many ordinary British people supported the operation, whereas a majority favoured the Iraq war only – and understandably enough, out of loyalty – for a brief moment when British forces went into action.

Even then, Eden could not say he wasn't warned. On the contrary, he was reminded in friendly but very forceful terms of the sheer unwisdom of 'the use of force' against an Arab country – which would, 'it seems to me, vastly increase the area of jeopardy'. This writer was President Dwight Eisenhower, in the days when things were different in the White House and the Republican Party. If Eden persevered in his folly, Ike wrote to the Prime Minister on 3 September 1956, not only the peoples of the Middle East but 'all of Asia and Africa would be consolidated against the West to a degree which, I fear, could not be overcome in a generation'. It would have been very fitting if Blair had quoted those words back to Bush forty-six years later.

Do we have national interests?

Within months of the invasion, nothing resembling the fabled 'WMD' had come to light and it was already clear that the ostensible reasons given had been false, even if at that point those ostensible reasons had not yet been, as they later would be, not merely falsified but stood on their heads. Blair could do no more than retreat into bluster and denial, and he then tried to change the subject, as so often before, but only dug himself into a deeper hole. We might not have found evidence of WMD, he said, but we had found other evidence, of mass graves: there was reason to think that Saddam had killed up to 300,000 people.

Nearly four years later, perhaps not many will remember where he was when he said that. He was in China, as the guest of a regime which, since the Communists took power in 1949, had killed not 300,000 but as many as seventy million people. What Saddam had done to the Kurds was horrible, but it was trivial compared to what the Chinese had done in Tibet. Why had we never gone to war with China?

All other arguments for the invasion were collapsing. Four years earlier Blair had impressed many people with his Chicago speech, which won 'the leader of the free world' so much acclaim. He had outlined the conditions to be met before any intervention:

> First, are we sure of our case? . . . Second, have we exhausted all diplomatic options? . . . Third, on the basis of a practical assessment of the situation, are there military operations we can sensibly and prudently undertake? Fourth, are we prepared for the long term? In the past we talked too much of exit strategies. But having made a commitment we cannot simply walk away once the fight is over . . . And finally, do we have national interests involved?

All of that was well put. And a question remained for Blair as the war spiralled out of control. Were all of those conditions met in the case of Iraq? Was any?

As to what Blair's real motives had been, an answer began to take shape. More than a year earlier he told one trusted journalist, Philip Stephens of the *Financial Times*, that he was worried about an American drift toward unilateralism and that his mission was to embrace Bush so tightly as to 'keep the United States in the international system'. Then some months before the war, he outlined to another, Peter Stothard, the former editor of the *Times*, his appreciation of the situation. Saddam Hussein was a danger to his enemies, who included the United States and Great Britain; 'not the only threat, but he was a threat nevertheless' (true in the broadest sense, though that did not make him a 'serious and current' threat to British interests as Blair had told Parliament). The American people, still traumatised by 11 September, would support a war on Iraq (also true enough) and such a war 'would happen whatever anyone else said or did' (just how true that was Blair knew very well).

And then came the crucial words, 'It would be more damaging to long-term world peace and security if the Americans alone defeated Saddam Hussein than if they had international support to do so.' This was extraordinarily candid, more than Blair may have realised. He knew the Americans were going to attack, and he believed that it would be better if we supported them regardless of the merits of the case. Blair's self-declared principle was not 'My country right or wrong' (which is bad enough) but 'Their country right or wrong'.

If this had been openly debated at the time, it would have been clear just how curious Blair's logic was. You don't say, 'My big brother is a crazy kind of guy. On

Saturday night he likes to get blind drunk and drive through town at ninety. It would be more damaging to peace and security if he acted alone than if he had my support, so I'll go along with him for the ride.' Either Washington was doing something wise and virtuous, in which case it should have been supported for that reason, or something foolish and vicious, in which case it should have been restrained and, if necessary, opposed.

The greatest flaw of all in Blair's position was pointed out by Cook in his resignation speech: the war would not be taking place if Al Gore were in the White House. That was certainly true – as a latter-day critic of the war, poor Al discovered a passion and eloquence which had quite eluded him when he was running for President – and confirms the point made earlier, that the decision for war was in effect taken by the Supreme Court. As to binding the Bush administration into the international order, judge for yourself.

Just as Suez ended Anthony Eden's career, so Iraq would have ended Blair's in an honest age. But there was one absolutely crucial difference. When all is said and all condemnations are made, Suez could in the end be defended in terms of the British national interest. And Blair's participation in the Iraq war cannot be, not in any honest way whatever. However misguided, Eden was still a national leader and not 'the Prime Minister of the United States' – or what one Beirut newspaper called Blair, 'Washington's international gofer'. Not that he cared. As he said, in words weirder and scarier still, 'I may be wrong but that is what I believe.'

Our greatest Prime Minister

Only one way

When did Tony Blair lose it? That everyday phrase covers a variety of meanings and a multitude of sins. We might ask when Blair lost his way, lost the war in Iraq, lost the plot, lost the respect of his colleagues, lost the trust of the British people, lost all moral authority, lost his grasp on reality, or lost his reason. Maybe the last can be dated to some time between late 2003 and late 2004.

His career had been punctuated by grandiloquent phrases, none of which wears well. 'A thousand days to prepare for a thousand years . . . I feel the hand of history on our shoulders . . . The kaleidoscope is shaken . . . I want not just to win your vote, but to win your heart and mind . . . We will stay with you to the last . . . Be prepared to be judged by history.' At the 2003 Labour conference he surpassed himself. Staring ahead in his prophetic manner, and in a voice quivering with insincere sincerity and empty profundity, he said, 'I can only go one way. I've not got a reverse gear.' This was a conscious echo of Margaret Thatcher's 'The lady's not for turning' (not her own finest oratorical hour), but it was far and away more foolish, one of the silliest things any national leader has ever said. Most motor vehicles have a reverse gear, and very useful it is; when you find yourself driving the wrong way up a one-way street, a reverse gear is not so much useful as essential.

Then again the phrase may have been all too accurate. Blair really does not have a reverse gear. However bad the mistakes he has made, he cannot admit that he has been wrong; he cannot change course even when it's obvious that he is heading for greater disaster. And now, pressing on in top gear, he ignored the unfolding catastrophe he had helped wreak.

He still had a few stalwart defenders, exhibiting a different kind of denial. Right up until the end of his premiership Blair has regularly been called the most successful leader Labour has ever had. In the autumn of 2006, John Prescott called him 'our greatest Prime Minister ever', although it wasn't clear whether he meant Labour premiers or the lot, and that Blair was greater than Pitt or Peel, Gladstone or Disraeli, Lloyd George or Churchill. Never one to be outdone in obsequious loyalty, Sir Gerald Kaufman said in a revealing phrase that 'we should go down on our knees' to thank Blair for all he had done.

These tributes are interesting. Those who made them could only be saying that politics is about winning elections, holding office, drawing salaries, and nothing else. Blair is the greatest Labour leader because he is the only one who has won three consecutive elections, not because of what he has done with those victories; the purpose of New Labour was office for its own sake and doing everything possible after each election to ensure re-election rather than to better the country.

In tuth, even as an electioneer Blair's record is less impressive than it might seem. He has won those three general elections, but by default, facing an unelectable Tory Party, and thanks to the distortions of the electoral system. Under his leadership Labour's popular vote has gone from 13.5 million to 10.7 million to 9.6 million, which scarcely suggests lasting enthusiasm on the part of the electorate. Blair never managed to equal John Major's 14 million votes in 1992, or even the 13.9 million Labour won under Attlee in 1951 (when Labour were robbed, with fewer MPs than the Tories but substantially more votes) from an electorate seven million smaller than in 1997.

In his first election Blair won fewer popular votes than Major had five years before; in his second, fewer than Labour had under Neil Kinnock in 1992; in his third, fewer than the Tories had in the debacle of 1997. These statistical curiosities are largely explained by the collapse in turnout between 1997 and 2001, but then that collapse is one of Blair's greatest political achievements. Fewer and fewer people want to vote, because politics means less and less to them and they despise politicians more and more, understandably enough. It's not that the British people think that they have an honest government led by a Prime Minister who tells the truth; they know that they have a deeply dishonest government led by a Prime Minister who habitually lies, and they don't care. That is Blair's victory.

One thing Blair has done is finally to make the case for electoral reform. He has won two huge parliamentary majorities, and one clear one, with the votes of well under a third, then under a quarter, and finally just over a fifth of the whole electorate. A rough-justice argument could once be made for the first-past-the-post Westminster electoral system in terms of clean breaks and stable governments, even when a party won 64 per cent of the parliamentary seats with 43 per cent of the vote, as in

1997; for a party to win 54 per cent of the seats with 35 per cent of the vote, as in 2005, is simply indefensible.

This book makes no pretence to examine the entire record of the Blair government. Obviously the economic record has been in many ways impressive, building on the work of the last Tory government and of Kenneth Clarke as Chancellor. Brown took one decision too Thatcherite for Thatcher when he handed over control of interest rates to an independent body, and this played an important part in that achievement – an unprecedented combination of low inflation, unemployment and interest rates with steady growth, of which Brown repetitiously reminds us. What he can't quite say, though many economists now do, is that the other reason for these achievements is the United Kingdom's remaining outside the single currency. As so often, governments sway from planned failure to unplanned success.

But the government's record has otherwise been patchy. Rather than assert that, let me adduce two journalists who have known Blair longer and better than most and strongly supported his early leadership of the Labour Party. On the tenth anniversary of that leadership Robert Harris only part-ironically saluted a man who had remained Prime Minister even though

he has alienated Labour's natural allies in Europe. British membership of the euro – once a cherished goal – is seemingly now so remote as to be barely worth discussion. On crime, education and health, he has shamelessly filched the rhetoric – and in some cases even the policies – of his Tory opponents . . .

Right-wing in his instincts even before he became party leader, Blair has clearly moved further to the right since entering Downing Street.

And Polly Toynbee, who has supported the government despite a foreign policy she dislikes, morosely thinks that the National Health Service – worshipped with almost superstitious reverence as the greatest of historic Labour achievements – 'risks becoming Labour's Iraq on the home front. The history of Labour's "reforms" hardly bears repeating; minister after minister reversed direction, created then tore up ten-year plans, dismantled then resurrected a market the party inherited.'

One other witness is still more telling, because he writes from afar and with academic detachment from our partisan passions. As I was finishing this book I happened to see the outline of a PhD dissertation entitled 'The Political Economy of Crisis Making: the United Kingdom from Attlee to Blair' by Matthias Matthijs, a young Belgian scholar now in the European Studies Department of Johns Hopkins University in Washington. His purpose is to explain why Blair, 'supported by a new body of Third Way ideas' and sustained by a huge parliamentary majority, 'did not achieve a major break with the Thatcherite settlement, but ended up strengthening it instead'. And he asks this comparative question:

Why were Attlee and Thatcher so successful in imposing many of their economic ideas and thus in changing the reigning political-economic consensus in Whitehall? And why were Heath and Blair, although both coming to power with fresh and coherent economic platforms, not able to translate their ideas into concrete government policy?

The Prime Minister likes to say that that history will be his judge. Well, here is one unusually intelligent historian, who was not even born when Blair was at Oxford, making a devastating judgement.

Much of this failure stems from Blairism's intellectual incoherence. Blair likes to boast that he is beyond ideology but if you have no coherent beliefs your practical politics will be a mess. If the only test is 'what works' then very likely nothing will work. If you try to please everyone then you may end up pleasing no one. Once again, the left have failed to grasp this. They grumble about Blair's obsession with the free market, which leads to his beloved private finance initiatives and public–private partnerships. But what's wrong with PFIs and PPPs is not they are too capitalistic or free-enterprising but that they are rip-offs which defraud the taxpayer.

In the end, and when the best case is made for it, the Blair regime cannot possibly be compared with the great radical reforming governments of the past: the Liberals in 1905–15, Labour in 1945–51, or before that the first Gladstone government in 1868–74, and indeed after that the Thatcher government in 1979–90. All of those changed the political weather, changed society, changed the country. The Blair government has at best played a modest consolidating role. And it is likely to be remembered for all that's most superficial, for abolishing the traditional practices of Parliament, for abolishing the traditional office of the Lord Chancellor, and for abolishing the traditional sport of fox-hunting.

That last, regardless of any rights or wrongs, says a great deal about Blair and his relations with his party, and about British political life today. There was that early, riveting moment when Blair said quite falsely that he had voted to ban hunting. There is the contrast between the more than 700 hours of parliamentary time which were devoted to the hunting ban and the seven hours which Parliament spent on the decision to invade Iraq. And there was a further connexion between the two. On the evening the ban was passed, Martha Kearney, a well-informed political journalist, spoke on *Newsnight* about the government's motives in reintroducing the Bill, and said quite matter-of-factly, 'it was brought back to restore morale after the war in Iraq'. So there it is. Labour MPs who had voted for a disastrous war few of them really wanted and whose hands were dripping with blood thought that they could wash the blood way by banning an esoteric rural sport.

When in ruminative mood, Blair says that constitutional reform may perhaps be his greatest legacy, but this only shows again how weak is his grip on reality. His government's record in this regard has been one of hesitation and cowardice leading to confusion and failure, epitomised by Blair's first attempt to do away with the Lord Chancellor, which was such a fiasco that Ferdinand Mount suggested it should be commemorated as National Cock-Up Day.

Not even the most grovelling Blairite 'loyalist' could defend the story of the House of Lords in the past ten years. There was a case for leaving the Lords untouched as an amusing relic, there was a case for root-and-branch reform and an elected second chamber, there was even a case for simply doing away with the Upper House. There was no case at all for the series of confused bungles and botched compromises which is all that the Blair government has achieved.

According to conventional wisdom, devolution for Scotland and Wales has been a success, but has it, at any rate from Blair's own perspective? Labour was a late, reluctant and cynical convert to the cause of devolution. The object of the exercise was entirely tactical and unprincipled: to hold off the nationalist challenge in Scotland, and to a lesser extent in Wales, while retaining as many as possible of Labour's Celtic rotten boroughs. In his early days Blair was not even sure whether the number of Scottish seats at Westminster would be reduced after devolution, saying different things about this to different people, but Blairites insisted – I well remember being told this by Peter Mandelson with every appearance of conviction – that devolution would strengthen the Union.

And the outcome? The 'West Lothian question' is unresolved, so that Scottish MPs at Westminster have little to do except vote on English legislation and collect their salaries and colossal expenses: the recent record-holder has been the preposterous 'loyalist' Eric Joyce, the MP for Falkirk, pocketing almost £175,000 a year in exes. Then last year, for the first time ever, a majority of Scots said in opinion polls that they wanted full independence, which would be a catastrophe for Labour. Once more Blair has shown a gift for short-term expediency regardless of long-term consequences.

To make it worse, Blair joyfully seized the excuse of terrorism and security to increase the assault on civil liberties and the rule of law, for which more than anything apart from Iraq his government will be remembered. It is a subject which deserves a book of its own, but it goes well beyond the intrusion of the surveillance state, with far more cameras watching us in this country than in any other on earth, so that four million out of thirty million CCTVs in operation globally are on British soil, photographing us up to 200 times a day, and, as in no other country, recording almost every journey made by every motor vehicle.

It goes beyond the insulting vexation of identity cards on which Blair has set his heart. ID cards were emblematic for him, not because of their utility, which is much debated, and despite their cost, which will be immense, but just to remind us who's in charge and of his commitment to the state against the individual, not to say his contempt for due process and individual freedom. It was said of that other Blair, Eric who became George Orwell, that he had an unusually high respect for truth and justice; Eric's namesake has an exceptionally low respect for them. This, after all, a man who once sneered at what he called 'libertarian nonsense'.

In the course of the Blair government, a thousand years of legal and forensic tradition have been discarded. Both the presumption of innocence and the burden of proof have ceased to be absolute principles, trial by jury has been curtailed, the right to silence is also gone and a judge may infer guilt from silence, hearsay evidence is admissible in court, and the rule against double jeopardy has been ended. The power of the state, which was frightening enough anyway, has been hugely extended by science. The police may now take and hold indefinitely DNA samples from anyone they arrest even if he is not charged or cautioned; and since 2006, for the first time ever, all offences are arrestable.

Like New Labour rhetoric, some innovations echo the age of totalitarianism. British citizens can be encarcerated without trial by means of anti-social behaviour orders, whose name echoes the proscription of 'social deviance' in the Third Reich; the government at one moment seriously proposed to make a 'disposition' towards terrorism an offence, just as those with a criminal disposition could be imprisoned in Germany under Hitler; and as Hazel Blears, a loyal Blairite minister, reminds us with admirable candour, 'Control orders are not designed to punish people for having done something wrong, but to prevent people from doing something wrong.'

Blair has been blamed by some and admired by others for destroying socialism. In truth the total eclipse of socialism at the end of the twentieth century was a great historical tide throughout the world which one Prime Minister could scarcely have achieved on his own. But Blair has indeed achieved something. By his endless war-making he has destroyed one English political tradition which had found a home in the Labour Party, the radical tradition of pacificism and non-interventionism; and by his attack on justice and freedom he has destroyed another, the liberal tradition. That is certainly a 'legacy'.

worse than, the occasion when the IRA stopped a bus in Armagh carrying ordinary working men, segregated Catholics from Protestants and killed all the Protestants?

His attempts to answer these conundrums have been both absurd and repellent. For one thing Blair said that he couldn't imagine the IRA killing 3,000 people, obviously intending 11 September. But if the IRA hadn't killed more people it wasn't for want of trying: their bomb in the City of London in 1992 might easily have killed hundreds if it had worked as intended and had exploded when the streets were crowded. In any case, if Blair had done a little basic maths he could have worked out that, proportionate to the respective populations of Northern Ireland and the United States, the IRA killed over the years the equivalent of 300,000 Americans, almost as many as the Americans who died in the Second Word War. Had that number been killed by a terrorist group, it is hard to imagine that Blair would have told the Americans that it was a trivial figure.

Worse still, Blair could only have been saying – if he had stopped to examine his own words – that murder was a statistical question and isn't so bad if fewer people are killed. Can he really think this? When he was a barrister, and if he had been defence counsel for a man accused of murder, would he have pleaded that the defendant had indeed killed a woman, but that another man had killed ten women and that therefore the defendant should be acquitted? Does he think that it was wrong for Hitler to have murdered a million Jewish children but that it would have been quite all right if he had only killed 20,000?

Going from bad to worse logically and ethically, Blair distinguishes between terrorists with rational and achievable aims and those without. 'I may agree or disagree with it' – the IRA's objective – 'but you can hardly say it is a demand that no sensible person can negotiate on.' But that can only mean that, if an objective is comprehensible and negotiable, it justifies terrorist murder. And the distinction is anyway specious. At the Downing Street press conference shortly after the 7 July attacks Blair became petulant when Michael White of the *Guardian* pointed out that a good deal of recent terrorist violence, in the Middle East and closer to home, has perfectly clear, practical and attainable objectives, notably the removal of Western forces from Iraq.

It suits Blair to portray Osama bin Laden as a maniac whose aims are mad as well as bad, and no doubt some of his objectives seem far fetched, even if restoring the caliphate is by no means more fantastical than Sinn Fein's ostensible aim of creating a united, socialist, Gaelic-speaking Irish republic. 'I don't think you can compare the political demands of republicanism with the political demands of this terrorist ideology we are facing now,' Blair says. Even if you disagree with the IRA's position, 'it is a demand that is shared by many of our citizens in the north', whereas al-Qaeda's aims 'are not demands any sensible person can negotiate on'.

At the time he spoke, much of the terrorist insurgency in Iraq was being directed by bin Laden's follower Abu Musab al-Zarqawi, later killed by American forces. Just as Adams wants to drive British troops out of Northern Ireland, al-Zarqawi wanted – as did the London suicide bombers – to drive American and British troops out of Iraq, murdering women and children in the process, like

Adams before him. And it's a fair bet that British soldiers will still be in Belfast when the last have left Basra.

By talking about 'a demand that is shared by many', Blair makes what his fellow barristers call a bad point, a disastrously bad one. Irish republicans want to undo the partition of Ireland which was effected by the creation of a separate province of Northern Ireland in 1920. To that end, the IRA engaged in terrorist murder; and that end, if not the means, is ostensibly supported by large numbers in Northern Ireland, the Irish Republic and America. Palestinian nationalists want to undo the partition of Palestine which was effected by the creation of a separate state of Israel in 1948. To that end, Palestinian groups have engaged in terrorist murder; and that end, if not the means, is undoubtedly supported by scores of millions of Arabs and Muslims. Why does their support not equally validate that objective?

This very comparison has been made by Ahmed Yousef, a senior adviser to the Palestinian Prime Minister, Ismail Haniya. Hamas is endlessly told that it must recognise Israel's right to exist but,

> after all, the Irish Republican Army agreed to halt its military struggle to free Northern Ireland from British rule without recognising British sovereignty. Irish Republicans continue to aspire to a united Ireland . . . had the IRA been forced to renounce its vision of reuniting Ireland before negotiations could occur, peace would never have prevailed. Why should more be demanded of the Palestinians, particularly when the spirit of our people will never permit it?

But all this is beside the point. Perhaps the real difference, for Blair as for his American sponsors, is that Gerry Adams is white.

From the high point of April 2003 until the catastrophes two years later, Blair's political and journalistic supporters began to drop away. Some Labour MPs made a parade of indignation that they had been misled, although that was surely to condemn themselves for their naivety at best. Others fell silent. What Blair himself said during this dismal phase deserves to be analysed by a team which would include an historian, a logician and a psychiatrist. Getting rid of Saddam was 'the right thing to do', Blair intones with repetitious circularity. 'If any part of the intelligence turns out to be wrong,' he said in February 2004, 'or if the threat from Saddam was different or changed from what we thought, I will accept this as I should, but let others accept that ridding Iraq of Saddam Hussein has made the world not just better but safer.'

As anyone else could see, the world was quite obviously not a safer place, but in any case, ridding Iraq of Saddam had specifically not been the object of the war, had it? Wasn't the object to disarm him of his dreadful weapons? 'We know Saddam Hussein had weapons of mass destruction but we know we haven't found them,' Blair told MPs in July 2004. 'I have to accept we have not found them, that we may not find them.' By this point he was almost gibbering.

Earlier the 'liberal hawks' had cheered him on, but their feet had now turned decidedly chilly. The writer and academic Michael Ignatieff, who last year returned to his native Canada and entered Parliament, had been a flag-waver when Baghdad fell but a year later was much disconcerted and dismayed by the failure to find weapons of mass destruction. He tried to re-examine the support he had once given Bush and Blair.

In hindsight, 'the honest case for war was "preventive" – to stop a tyrant with malignant intentions from acquiring lethal capabilities or transferring those capabilities to other enemies. The case we actually heard was "pre-emptive" – to stop a tyrant who already possessed weapons and posed an imminent danger.' That was fair enough, but Ignatieff then added glumly that 'the problem for my side is that if the honest case had been put – for a preventive as opposed to a pre-emptive war – the war would have been even more unpopular than it was'.

Well, quite. And that was an indirect admission that the way Blair had sold the war was always bound to be dishonest. Bush liked to say, at least early on, that Iraq had been 'a war of necessity', not choice. That was obviously untrue: no 'preventive war' is strictly necessary. While there might have been good reasons for the war, the reasons Blair gave could not have been good, because they weren't true. Nor could he have told the truth: he told a lie of necessity, not choice.

Epilogue: It's worse than you think

The intelligence was fixed

As the new year of 2007 opened it found two Englishmen far from home and far from happy. 'We tried our guts out,' Andrew Flintoff said, after a Test series in which the England cricket team he captained had just sustained the first 5-0 whitewash in nearly eighty-five years. 'It hasn't quite gone the way we'd like it to.' At least the cricketers hadn't endured the final ordeal of the British Lions rugby players in the summer of 2005. Hired as media adviser by Clive Woodward, the Lions manager, Alastair Campbell had resorted to his usual methods, bullying and blackguarding players and causing intense ill feeling within the team. 'Not for Clan Campbell the loser's mentality that participation is as important as winning,' he wrote in his infinitely risible sports column; when the All Blacks crushingly won the three-match series 21-3, 48-18 and 38-19 it was maybe a small mercy that Campbell of the Dodgy Dossier didn't claim this as a brilliant victory for the Lions.

Although Flintoff's words were comically meiotic, he was at any rate more honest than Tony Blair, who was far from admitting that things hadn't gone the way he would have liked. He sat in Palm Beach in the home of a pop singer, Robin Gibb of the Bee Gees. Downing Street said that it was a commercial letting rather than another

Blairite freebie, but the commercial rate for this Florida gin palace would be tens of thousands a week. Were the Blairs really paying?

Even when he returned to London, Blair had nothing at all to say about the great event of the moment, the execution of Saddam Hussein, a hanging more like a lynching, filmed in front of jeering enemies and then shown around the world. At Suez, Conor Cruise O'Brien once dryly observed, the British and French had attempted the tricky feat of destroying the most popular of Arab leaders without forfeiting Arab support; now an even harder feat was being achieved, of turning a mass murderer into a hero and martyr.

In response to that repulsive spectacle, George W. Bush said that it was 'an important milestone', which it certainly was for Saddam, and it was after all only one more execution to go with the 152 over which Bush had presided in Texas. In London three of Blair's colleagues, John Prescott, Lord Falconer and then Gordon Brown, all publicly expressed their revulsion, but the Prime Minister refused to say anything. That long silence was all the more striking since Blair has never been reticent about matters of life and death. On many occasions he affected instant sorrow at the demise of some well-known personage: interrupting an economic summit to say how much Frank Sinatra had meant to him ('I grew up with him'); demanding, in the course of an ostensibly serious political statement, the release from prison of a character in the television soap *Coronation Street*; or condemning the manager of the England football team – who duly lost his job – for the expression of personal religious opinions.

After ten days finally Blair admitted that 'the manner of the execution of Saddam was completely wrong'. Even then he had to add, 'that should not blind us to the crimes he committed against his own people, including the death of hundreds of thousands of innocent Iraqis, one million casualties in the Iran–Iraq war and the use of chemical weapons against his own people, wiping out entire villages,' as if anyone was defending those crimes.

Over this weird final phase, Blair's career is no longer merely a case of 'in office but not in power'; he is only notionally in office, and more and more seems a shadowy figure in the bunker, moving imaginary armies on a map. He complains about every aspect of public services – and not without reason given the state of the NHS, the latest education figures, the decay of public transport, or a disintegrating Home Office 'not fit for purpose' – but all as though he had no idea who had been governing the country for the past ten years. The man who once wanted 'a thousand days to prepare for a thousand years' now demands ten-year plans to be drawn up by his Cabinet ministers, unaware that they are all twiddling their thumbs as they wait for him to go, knowing that any such plans intended for his eyes will be waste paper in a few months' time.

His fantasy life is shared by his little entourage, as we were reminded by the utterly ludicrous – but quite genuine – memo about plans for his departure which was leaked last autumn, in which his preposterous sycophantic courtiers hope for a 'farewell tour' to promote the 'triumph of Blairism'. As Blair 'enters his final phase he needs to be focusing way beyond the finishing line, not looking at it'. It was proposed that, on this last tour, the Prime Minister should 'be seen with people who will raise eyebrows', which evidently meant appearing on *Blue Peter*, *Songs of Praise* and Chris Evans's radio show. 'He must go with the crowds wanting more', as a 'star who won't even play that last encore'.

This would be very funny, if it hadn't been for what was actually happening in Iraq, where the execution of Saddam and then two of his lieutenants (one of whom was beheaded by the noose) heightened the cycle of violence and vengeance, with scores of Shiites hanged from lampposts in Baghdad. In Washington, Bush had already summoned a group of elder statesmen to deliberate on the calamity but, having heard their advice, chose not to take it. Instead he proposed a 'surge' or commitment of fresh troops to try and restore order in Baghdad, in the very optimistic belief that this might be a prelude to orderly departure. But this decision, right or wrong, was plainly taken by Bush without even pretending to consult Blair or to consider British interests.

And in London there was a great void. Years ago in the Commons, the late George Brown once responded haughtily that he proposed 'to treat that remark with a complete ignoral'; Blair now treats the Iraq catastrophe with an ignoral. There was of course no possibility of increasing the number of British troops, as the armed forces were now overstretched at every point, notably in an Afghanistan where allied forces confront another defeat. In fact, Blair's ministers made it clear that our soldiers would be withdrawn from Iraq as soon as possible, whatever the consequences, and as if nothing that happened to the country thereafter would be any of our responsibility.

Even worse, Blair had managed to impose his ignoral on Parliament, which was too bored and too guilty to call him to account. Like those who elected them, most MPs were longing for Blair to go away, and were ready to follow his favourite words and draw a line under the Blair prime ministership and move on, although that meant overlooking the huge discredit his reign had brought on politics and politicians as a whole.

This may be the bitterest irony of all, apart from the way that (in one more echo of Vietnam) in order to liberate Iraq it was first necessary to destroy it. Both the great legislatures, at Westminster and on Capitol Hill, had succumbed to vulgar bullying and blatant mendacity, abdicating a specific constitutional right to declare war in the case of Congress, voting for a war which in their hearts they disliked and should have opposed in the case of the Commons, and had shamefully neglected their duty to hold the executive to account. And so, in order hypothetically or in theory to bring democracy to Mesopotamia, democracy was gravely damaged where it already existed: in the country which had given the world parliamentary government, and in the country which had given the world government of the people, by the people, for the people.

Not only Parliament but the British electorate had allowed Blair to remain in office even as evidence of his shameful culpability had grown all the time: if his political coffin was not yet firmly closed, it wasn't for want of nails. Two had been hammered home in the spring of 2005,

137

when immensely important and damning pieces of evidence came to light, dating from three years earlier. Either should have finished Blair, let alone both. For one, it transpired that he had sought an opinion about the legality of an invasion of Iraq as early as April 2002, on his return from visiting Bush in Crawford, confirming that the war was being planned then.

Still more devastating was the 'Downing Street memo'. It was dated 23 July 2002, written by Matthew Rycroft, a Downing Street official, addressed to David Manning, then Blair's senior foreign policy adviser, subsequently ambassador in Washington, and copied to the Defence Secretary, Geoff Hoon; the Foreign Secretary, Jack Straw; the Attorney-General, Lord Goldsmith; the Cabinet Secretary, Sir Richard Wilson; John Scarlett of the Joint Intelligence Committee; 'C', or Richard Dearlove, head of MI6; Jonathan Powell, Blair's chief of staff; and Alastair Campbell, who needs no introduction: 'all the conspirators save only he', and that 'he', the Prime Minister, knew better than anyone what the memo said.

At the heart of this 'extremely sensitive' document ('No further copies should be made. It should be shown only to those with a genuine need to know.') was a summary of the American position after secret talks in Washington; I shall italicise the most lethal passages.

There was a perceptible shift in attitude. *Military action was now seen as inevitable.* Bush wanted to remove Saddam, through military action, justified by the conjunction of terrorism and WMD. *But the intelligence and facts were being fixed around the policy.* The NSC

[American National Security Council] had no
patience with the UN route, and no enthusiasm for
publishing material on the Iraqi regime's record. *There
was little discussion in Washington of the aftermath after
military action.*

The memo also recorded the Attorney-General's
opinion that 'regime change was not a legal base for
military action', and Blair's that if 'the political context
were right, people would support regime change'. In any
case, '*We should work on the assumption that the UK would take
part in any military action.*' In America, the memo caused
a sensation: Congressman John Conyers sent a letter to
President Bush signed by eighty-nine Democratic
colleagues in Congress demanding an inquiry. By contrast, it fell flat in Blair's country, which no longer cared
about any lies told.

Any further doubt that there was 'something truly
loathsome about the modern Labour Party' had been
ended by two grotesque moments in the election campaign that spring. Blair appeared on television to be grilled
by 'Little Ant and Dec', two unbearable ten-year-olds,
smirking as they asked him 'Have you always been that
bossy?', 'Are you mad?' (good questions, it might be said)
and 'If you make an ugly smell, do people pretend not to
notice because you're Prime Minister?'. Afterwards Blair
confided that 'it's always a battle' between 'the modern
world in which we live ... and the dignity of the office'.

As if to emphasise the point, he and Cherie gave an
interview to their favourite newspaper, the *Sun*, in which
he 'joked he was a "five times a night" man. "At least, I

can do it more depending how I feel."' Was he really up to it, asked the *Sun*. '"He always is!" Cherie replied.' Although 'five times a night Tony' became a transient joke (or 'another Labour lie', one Tory cynic said), the episode was in its way decisive. After that interview in which the Blairs so repulsively invaded their own privacy, no politician in Blair's government or party could ever again in any circumstances whatever complain about invasion of privacy.

Other Prime Ministers before now might have boasted of their sexual potency, David Lloyd George among them. The comparisons between him and Blair are provocative, none telling in Blair's favour, quite apart from the fact that Lloyd George led the country to victory in war. That 'atmosphere of intrigue and corruption' for which the Lloyd George government had been notorious was truer of the Blair government all the time, until the amazing day at the end of 2006 when the Prime Minister was interrogated by the police at Downing Street about the sale of honours.

And the same day also heard Lord Goldsmith, the Attorney-General, he who had conveniently changed his mind about the legality of the Iraq war, say that he had suppressed an investigation into bribery connected with arms sales to Saudi Arabia: 'It has been necessary to balance the need to maintain the rule of law against the wider public interest.' This was New Labour, which was going to be 'whiter than white'; a government which would add 'an ethical dimension to foreign policy'.

Even more blatantly than Blair, Lloyd George provided honours to political donors, and he was said to have been the first Prime Minister since Walpole to leave office flagrantly richer than he entered it, whereas Blair leaves Downing Street not richer but much more heavily indebted. But the distinction may be illusory, and nothing like enough attention has been devoted to Blair's financial life. For all the criticism made of the British media, sometimes with justice, newspapers are capable of showing restraint. The Prime Minister and his wife themselves know that very well, from the time when the press was asked not to mention a Blair family drama and duly kept complete silence, so that every journalist knows about an incident the larger public never heard of.

And yet, if it was right to observe that silence, then it is entirely proper to speculate about the Blairs' income and property transactions, past and future. Before 1997 they owned a house in a pleasant part of Islington which they could perfectly well have let while they lived at Downing Street and Chequers, but Campbell, obsessed as usual with news management, and concerned about a trivial scandal when a Tory politician had let a flat to a disreputable tenant, told them to sell it. This was one of the worst pieces of advice even he ever gave, since the house would have hugely appreciated in value over the next ten years, and this has added to the Blairs' bitterness about their comparative impoverishment alongside their successful contemporaries.

Then Cherie Blair bought two flats in Bristol, one for her son to live in while he was at university and one as a nest egg, which is to say that the wife of a Labour Prime Minister was engaged in property speculation. She used, moreover, the services of a man who had managed the unlikely feat of being imprisoned for fraud in three different continents. He was the former lover of Cherie's bizarre friend Carole Caplin, who had already been charging the Blairs a large sum for 'lifestyle' and fashion advice. To judge from an unforgettable photograph of Cherie and Carole at the Chelsea Flower Show, wearing spangled catsuits and pixie boots and looking like nothing so much as a pair of trapeze artists, the money was not well spent.

But even if she doesn't have much taste in clothes, Cherie Blair certainly likes them. On a visit to Australia, she was asked by the owner of a clothing shop if she would like to take a couple of things as presents, and took sixty-eight, from jeans and jumpers to pyjamas and underwear. And it was in Australia that she had also required a fee of £100,000 for speaking on behalf of a cancer charity. This thirst for money has lurked in the background for many years, a thread running through the Prime Minister's dealings with the shadowy figure of Lord Levy and the purchase of a house in Connaught Square, close to Marble Arch.

Once again the Blairs seem to have been badly advised and paid over the odds. They were obliged to raise a mortgage of nearly £3.5 million, on top of mortgages of more than £450,000 for the Bristol flats. Having earlier declined to accept his full salary, Blair began in 2001 to receive the full Prime Minister's salary, now £187,000. And yet the whole of that, even before tax, wouldn't begin to service those mortgages, and even if Cherie's income at the Bar is substantially higher it is hard to see how they can afford the house.

One answer may be America, another Rupert Murdoch. There can be little doubt at all that Blair will head westwards when he leaves office. If the House of Lords is 'not my style', the lucrative American lecture circuit surely is. The going rates for retired politicians are impressive, ranging from $60,000 an evening for Madeleine Albright up to $250,000 for Bill Clinton, and Blair will be at the high end of the scale. On top of that is what he will get for his memoirs and any other books he may write, or employ someone to write for him.

In all the years since Blair's first visit to the News Corp celebration in Australia, no one has ever got to the bottom of his relationship with Murdoch, but it's very intimate. The Blair years saw the rise of the 'sofa government' that so dismayed a mandarin of the old school such as Lord Butler. With Parliament treated like the Supreme Soviet, and the Cabinet like the Politburo, the country has in effect been ruled over these years by a cabal of six people, with Powell and Campbell in practice far more powerful than most elected politicians. They and one other: the former Downing Street media officer Lance Price has said that Murdoch always seemed to be the twenty-fourth member of the Cabinet, and the formidable magnate sat invisibly beside Blair on the sofa.

Some of the Prime Minister's telephone conversations are logged at Downing Street, though not all. We know for example that he spoke to Murdoch on 13 March 2003; the following day, Blair's line on Iraq was faithfully parroted in the Murdoch press from the *Times* ('The prospects for a peaceful solution to the crisis have been undermined by French intransigence and Saddam Hussein's belligerence') all the way up to the *Sun*. Shortly thereafter the government dismissed the demand for a 'plurality test' which David Puttnam and others in the Lords were trying to insert in the Communications Bill, which would have impeded further acquisitions of television channels by Murdoch. And a year later came Blair's farcical about-turn on the European constitution referendum as a sweetener for Murdoch.

Why should this beautiful friendship not bear further fruit? One way of paying off a politician is a book contract. A huge sum is advanced, far more than the book can possibly earn, but then plenty of us are familiar with the words 'unearned advance' on a statement. Blair deserves to be watched very closely indeed after he leaves office, to see just what post-dated quid there will be pro quo.

In America, for no good reason, Blair has escaped much of the obloquy directed at Bush, and the Prime Minister remains more popular there than he does at home, a response to his adoring embrace. Although he has been awarded the Congressional gold medal he has not yet thought it prudent to accept it, but that will no doubt come soon after he leaves office. Blairmania may have receded from its giddy heights of four years ago, when the President said that 'I'm proud to call him friend' and the *New York Daily News* shouted 'God Save Tony Blair', but something of that aura lingers. Jacques Chirac and Gerhard Schroeder opposed the Iraq war, and what is either of them now worth on the American lecture trail? And what would Blair be worth if he too had opposed it? Sweet are the uses of adversity. Vast numbers of lives may have been cruelly ruined by the Iraq enterprise, but Tony Blair will surely be a richer man as a result.

Tony Blair doesn't even have respect

In a hallowed Fleet Street story, a correspondent posted to some far-flung, strife-torn spot began a despatch to his foreign desk in London, 'It would be difficult to exaggerate the horror of events unfolding here, but I shall do my best.' His eloquence would be unnecessary in Iraq today. It's not so much difficult as well-nigh impossible to describe the horror that has unfolded since the invasion four years ago.

A mark of this disaster is that no one really knows how bad it is. Large parts of Iraq are inaccessible and no reporter can enter them and come out alive. We have no accurate idea how many people have died: certainly 60,000, probably 100,000, very likely more, perhaps many more. At least a twelfth of the population has fled the country, including most of the educated middle class, the people that starry-eyed supporters of the invasion insisted would turn Iraq overnight into a thriving democracy.

Not only has every prophecy made by such optimists been horribly confounded, not only has every justification Blair gave been shown to be a falsehood, every one of them has been stood on its head. There were no 'weapons of mass destruction' in Iraq; but there was a great deal of dangerous weaponry which went missing and has since been used with hideous effect. Saddam was not connected with 11 September or with violent Islamism in general – he was a brutal tyrant, but a brutal secular tyrant, who had a very short way with such zealots – and there were no fundamentalist terrorists in Iraq five years ago; but now the country is awash with them. In another of his deluded orations, Blair told the Labour conference in the autumn of 2004 that 'Iraq was not a safe country before March 2003', as though that was the point. Does even he think it is a safer country today?

Then there was the great cause of bringing democracy to Iraq. Predictably enough, the results of democratic elections have been everything that Blair didn't want, and in August of last year, the *New York Times* learned from someone who had just been at a private White House briefing that the administration 'have acknowledged to me that they are considering alternatives other than democracy'. As violence exploded again following Saddam's execution, the wretched Nouri al-Maliki said that he no longer wanted to be Prime Minister, and had never wanted to be in the first place. Who can blame him? The poor fellow simply doesn't share Blair's ambition, lack of conscience and capacity for evasion.

As a last resort there was the humanitarian argument: Saddam was a brute who killed many innocent people. And yet, as various human-rights bodies have pointed out, his despotism, though always harsh, was much less sanguinary in its later years than earlier, and without question far more Iraqis have died in the four years since the invasion than in the four years before it. If oppression had been the issue, then the time to have invaded Iraq would have been twenty years earlier, when Saddam was butchering the Kurds, although that was unfortunately also the time when the British government was selling him whatever arms he wanted, when Washington supported his war against Iran, and when Donald Rumsfeld was a honoured guest in Baghdad.

In polite circles, 'conspiracy theory' is an insult, but in the case of Iraq, the conspiracy theories – was it really a war for oil? was it really a war for Israel? – are almost flattering since they might have made some kind of sense as motives for the invasion, which is more than can be said for most of the ostensible reasons. We have seen Murdoch saying that 'the greatest thing to come out of this for the world economy, if you could put it that way, would be $20 a barrel for oil', while there were important figures in the Bush administration who had previously worked for Benjamin Netanyahu and Likud, and who gave every appearance of being at least as devoted to the interests of Israel as of the United States.

Suppose that those really were motives, how far have they been gratified? Yuval Diskin is head of Shin Bet, the Israeli domestic security service. When he spoke in private early last year to a group of army recruits his words were surreptitiously recorded and broadcast on television. It could be that they would come to regret the overthrow of the tyrant, Diskin said. Brutal as his rule was, it might have been less dangerous for Israel than the chaos which had succeeded him: 'I'm not sure we won't miss Saddam.' As for 'the world economy', as I write – and as Murdoch has probably noticed – the price of oil is $52 a barrel.

It would be tedious and fruitless to rub this in if it weren't for Blair's psychotic inability to admit that he was wrong. 'History will be my judge,' he likes to say in another of his unhappy echoes: as Hitler told the Munich court in 1924, 'It is not you, gentlemen, who pass judgment on us. That judgment is spoken by the eternal court of history.' Well, it is being spoken.

More and more Americans have come to share the view of the eminent historian Sean Wilentz that George Bush the Younger must now be reckoned the worst President in his country's history. The United States is quite obviously much weaker, politically, diplomatically, economically, even militarily, than when Bush was inaugurated. That was when the Iraq war was first dreamed of, something confirmed by Richard Clarke, one of Bush's original colleagues.

On the last day of 2006, Clarke listed all the grave questions which had been neglected by the administration but which would have been addressed 'without the distraction of the Iraq war', from Russian revanchism to conflict in Africa, from the Latin American swing to the left to arms control or the lack of it, from the real threat represented by Al-Qaeda to global warming. Blair likes to flourish climate change as one subject where he differs from Bush, but then as Clarke says, whenever they meet, 'Iraq squeezes out the time to discuss the pending planetary disaster'.

That is precisely the point. On this as on every other matter, Blair's abject fealty has won him no influence of any kind whatever, and this finally demolishes his personal reason for supporting the war. 'It's worse than you think,' he likes to say: he really believed in the invasion. And yet that is at odds with his belief that 'it would be more damaging to long-term world peace and security if the Americans alone defeated Saddam Hussein' than if he joined in, and that by doing so he would 'keep the United States in the international system'. But the war has been immensely damaging to world peace and security; and as

to the idea of guiding or restraining the Bush administration, comment is superfluous. They have been guided
and restrained all the way from Guantanamo Bay to Abu
Ghraib, crimes in which Blair has made the British people
complicit.

Before the invasion Blair invoked 'the slums of Gaza',
but he has done nothing whatever for them, and his
adherence to Washington has helped to make a settlement
of the Israeli–Palestinian conflict more remote than ever.
However much Blair deludes himself, no British Prime
Minister can solve that problem. But he – or she – can at
least stand up straight. In 2006, Blair refused to condemn
the Israeli attack on Lebanon; twenty years earlier
Margaret Thatcher refused to support the Israeli attack on
the PLO headquarters in Lebanon. 'I do not believe in
retaliatory strikes that are against international law,' she
said, while wondering, as well she might, what the
American reaction would be if she had 'bombed the
Provos in Dundalk'.

In 1986 she also visited Washington. When she met
George Shultz, the Secretary of State, she gave him a
tongue-lashing which is recorded in the NSC archives. Did
Yitzhak Shamir, then the Israeli Prime Minister, ever
intend to negotiate over the West Bank and Jerusalem, she
asked? Israel was 'simply holding the world to ransom',
and couldn't claim to be the only democracy in the Middle
East while it 'denies basic rights' to the Palestinians.
Washington was the only power which could do anything
about this, Thatcher said, but instead it acquiesced in every
Israeli action.

At no time has Blair ever spoken like that in public, and

there is no reason to think that he has in private either. Hence the utter hypocrisy of his words about the people of Gaza; hence the utter absurdity of his visit to the Levant before Christmas 2006. As Marc Sirois of the Beirut *Daily Star* told the BBC at the time, Blair had abdicated any responsibility he ever had towards that conflict and couldn't possibly act as an honest broker, since

> he is identified so strongly by Arabs in general and Palestinians in particular as somebody who supports the policies of the Bush administration and the United States. [He has] sacrificed what credibility he ever had in this part of the world so his mission is in fact – I don't want to call it a fool's errand but there's nothing he can do . . . George Bush might be hated here but least he's respected. Tony Blair doesn't even have respect.

Nor in the end does he have any real respect in Washington, for all the backslapping of this 'friend': not respect that can be turned into anything practical. If he hadn't learned that after his insulting treatment in Washington in April 2004, there were the events of last summer when Alan Cowell, the perceptive London correspondent of the *New York Times*, observed that 'if the Lebanon conflict said anything about what some Britons like to call their special relationship with America, it seemed to be this: in this Middle East war, the only special relationship bound the United States to Israel, not Britain.'

Rather than acknowledge that, Blair retreats into more

denial and bluster. When David Cameron made a thoughtful speech about the one-sided Anglo-American relationship, Blair accused him of wanting to 'pander to anti-Americanism' by 'stepping back from America', and at the end of 2006 he said that if we gave up our 'strong relationship' with the United States then 'we will pay a very heavy price in the future'. Even he might have stopped to wonder if it could be any heavier than the price we have paid for his grovelling loyalty.

What emerges through the wreckage is the disparity between Blair's lofty rhetoric and his tiny achievements, between the public plaudits he received from Bush and the way Bush actually treated him, between his obsequious praise of America and the contemptuous requital. Look at the huge list of American books about Iraq.[1] While in America some months ago, I went through a pile of these books, without at first seeing where I was going, flipping and dipping as I looked for 'Blair, Tony' in the index or for any appearances by our Prime Minister in the text.

And then it dawned on me: like Sherlock Holmes's dog that didn't bark in the night, *he wasn't there.* His significance is his insignificance. In all of these well-researched and

[1] A selection would include James Fallows's *Blind into Baghdad* (Vintage, 2006), George Packer's *The Assassins' Gate* (Farrar, Straus and Giroux, 2005), Thomas E. Ricks's *Fiasco* (Penguin, 2006), Michael Gordon and General Bernard Trainor's *Cobra II* (Pantheon, 2006), Bob Woodward's *State of Denial* (Simon and Schuster, 2006), Ron Suskind's *The One Percent Doctrine* (Simon and Schuster, 2006), Michael Isikoff and David Corn's *Hubris* (Crown, 2006) and Rajiv Chandrasekaran's *Imperial Life in the Emerald City* (Knopf, 2006).

authoritative books, Blair scarcely appears even as a bit player or spear carrier; he ranks somewhere in importance between a long-serving Midwestern congressman and a deputy secretary of state. All this confirms what Sir Christopher Meyer says he learned as ambassador in Washington, that there are just three countries whose governments the White House takes seriously: Israel, Ireland and Saudi Arabia.

Other Americans agree, with varying degrees of rue or embarrassment. In a lecture last autumn, Kendall Myers, a senior State Department analyst, said that every British attempt to influence American policy had been pointless: 'we typically ignore them and take no notice'. He even felt 'a little ashamed' at the way Blair had been treated by Bush, after he had staked his career on supporting the White House: 'There was nothing. There was no payback, no sense of reciprocity.'

That is the nub of it. Another American, John Brady Kiesling, resigned from the foreign service in protest at the invasion. In his letter of resignation he asked: 'Has "*oderint dum metuant*" really become our motto?' and it was good to see that there were still American diplomatists who could muster a Latin tag, in this case Accius' phrase, which Caligula relished, 'Let them hate us so long as they fear us.' Such has indeed been the precept observed by Washington; but if the Bush administration follows Accius in its dealing with its acknowledged enemies, its watch-word towards its supposed friends has been taken from Prince Schwarzenberg: 'They will be astonished by our ingratitude.' Blair gave Bush everything, and got nothing in return.

At times this has seemed like Maoist 'ritual humiliation', and the relationship now takes the form of 'capitulations', as they were known when the European powers imposed their terms on the decaying Ottoman Empire. On all sides the evidence of Blair's failure, in his own terms, is overwhelming. When Washington wants a co-sponsor for a United Nations resolution it turns to France, generally recognised as an independent country, rather than the United Kingdom, seen throughout the world as no more than an American satellite. When Washington wants to work with a serious European leader it turns to Angela Merkel, the German Chancellor, and not to the British Prime Minister, whose only remaining use to the White House is to provide a little emotional support; as Maureen Dowd says, poor Bush huddles in the White House with no friends left except Barney and Tony, 'his Scotch terrier and his English poodle'.

Not only is the United States weaker today than when Bush was inaugurated, Great Britain is far weaker than in the bright dawn of 1997, while Blair himself is pitifully diminished. Eight years ago an American called Blair 'the leader of the free world'; could anyone possibly say that today? Only three years ago a London journalist wrote a book intended for American readers called *Tony Blair: The Making of a World Leader*; could a book of that title still be published without derision? He has certainly taught, and been taught, the limits of 'leadership', and now he leads nowhere and no one at all.

And Blair has taught another lesson without meaning to. His American flatterers used to compare him with great predecessors, a man 'in the spirit of Margaret

Thatcher and Winston Churchill', said the *New York Post* as the war began. But Thatcher was far less servile than Blair, and Churchill was far more honourable.

On 3 September 1939, the day that the greatest of wars began, Churchill told the Commons that 'our repeated efforts for peace' had all been ill starred, 'but all have been faithful and sincere. This is of the highest moral value . . . Outside, the storms of war may blow and the lands may be lashed with the fury of its gales, but in our hearts this Sunday morning there is peace. Our hands may be active, but our consciences are at rest.' More than a year later, by now Prime Minister, Churchill said again that every effort had been made to avoid war: 'Long and hard, hazardous years lie before us, but at least we entered upon them united and with clean hands.'

So much of the disaster of the past years stems from the awful truth that we did not enter upon Blair's war united, and that he did not have clean hands; if he has a conscience, it cannot possibly be at rest. But then 'if' may be the word. For all his parade of religious zeal, he seems incapable of contrition. A man who has apologised for everything from slavery to the Irish famine says that he 'will never apologise' for what he has done in Iraq, and to his own country. There is nothing left to tell him but Cromwell's words: 'Depart, I say, and let us have done with you. In the name of God, go!'